St. Monica
and the Power of
Persistent Prayer

St. Monica

and the Power of Persistent Prayer

Mike Aquilina and Mark W. Sullivan

Foreword by Lisa Hendey

Our Sunday Visitor Publishing Division
Our Sunday Visitor, Inc.
Huntington, Indiana 46750

Contents

Foreword

Hope for the Journey

By Lisa M. Hendey

I have St. Monica on speed dial. As the wife of a convert and a mother of two young adult sons, there are some days when I feel as though I'm carrying on a continual conversation with one of my favorite patron saints. Blessedly, I know that the same burning desire to share heaven one day with her own husband and children opens Monica's heart to this simple Fresno housewife.

I don't remember precisely when my fervent prayers for my husband's conversion first became a steady drumbeat in St. Monica's ears. I'll admit that when we married under the shadow of the golden dome at our *alma mater*, the University of Notre Dame's Basilica of the Sacred Heart, Greg's nominally Lutheran background wasn't as big an issue for me as it perhaps should have been. We entered our marriage with a starry-eyed agreement that our future children would be raised in the Catholic faith. At that point, I felt equal to the task, knowing that my husband — while not Catholic — was a "good person" and would at least be very supportive.

Although I spent many a Sunday alone at Mass with two maddeningly active toddlers, I don't think the reality of our situation truly hit me until our eldest son, Eric, began to prepare for the sacraments of Reconciliation and First Communion. As we readied ourselves for Eric's sacraments, my heart began to yearn for my husband's faithful presence with the boys and me. I wanted him *at* the Eucharistic table, not simply in the pew watching us receive. I began to turn to St. Monica regularly in prayer, asking that she intercede on behalf of my wonderful husband as she had done in her own marriage and with her own notoriously vagrant son, Augustine.

Interestingly, after seventeen years of marriage, my prayers began to morph away from my "wish list" for Greg, and more toward my own need for conversion. I asked St. Monica to be my spiritual companion in life — *just as it was dealt to me* — rather than expecting or holding my breath for a change in my husband. I prayed, through her intercession, for peace of heart, for the worthiness to be equal to the challenge of leading our domestic church, and for a grateful spirit to accept my husband's personal path to conversion. It was only after letting go of my agenda for things being done according to "Lisa's time" that God's plan unfurled. Greg and our younger son Adam both received their First Holy Communion three years later. My husband, now a Knight of Columbus and a liturgical music minister at our parish, is still learning about our Church and continuing along his path to salvation.

Greg's becoming Catholic through the Rite of Christian Initiation of Adults did not mark the end of my prayers to St. Monica. I recall sending her tearful prayers of thanksgiving that Easter Vigil night as I watched my husband being confirmed. But honestly, those same tears frequently flow with gratitude when I see the man I love receive the Eucharist on any given Sunday. Greg's faithfulness and his companionship along my own path to heaven are blessings I will never take for granted. And now, as we watch our sons grow into strong, independent men, it is St. Monica's passionate advocacy for her son St. Augustine that has me regularly coming together for a tête-à-tête with this intercessor. She knows the words of my heart without my even having spoken them.

From my vantage point as a Catholic blogger, I have had the opportunity to witness firsthand the devotion that so many have to St. Monica. Their combox stories and personal emails remind me on a daily basis that so many of us turn to St. Augustine's mom regularly for support and strength as we raise children in an increasingly secularized society. The "prayer intentions" folder I keep in my email inbox bulges with their accounts. They include:

"Mary," herself a convert to the faith who likens herself to Augustine in her own circuitous path home to the Church. Now, she turns to St. Monica's intercessory care for a son she calls "wayward."

"Laura," a one-time rebellious child, now a wife and mother, who invokes St. Monica's prayers on behalf of her husband's stubborn lack of faith.

"Thomas," a modern-day self-appointed Augustine, who, having come home to the Church, prays fervently for the

young men in his life who are adrift in a society awash in sexual sin and spiritual discouragement or oblivion.

"Seth," who now respects his own mother's consistent and loving prayers on his behalf during his rebellious years as he embarks upon his own parenting journey.

"Darlene," a mother of many, who continues to persevere in leading her domestic church alone after the untimely death of her spouse.

Their stories are real-world examples of the faith it sometimes takes to simply, faithfully put one foot in front of the other each day. They are the reason I'm so thrilled to now be able to share *St. Monica and the Power of Persistent Prayer* with my friends, readers, and loved ones. With this book, which is more an invitation to prayer and transformation than a simple "read it once and set it aside" volume, Mike and Mark offer support and encouragement for personal transformation.

The chapters of this book will help you come to better know St. Monica and St. Augustine through the liberal sharing of their words of wisdom. The early pages provide a look at their lives in the context of their time in history. These stories might as well come from a blockbuster film. They point to the saints' relevance today when so many of the issues they faced continue to plague us. As the book continues, Mike and Mark invite us into deeper dialogue, with meditations, resolutions, and prayer to enkindle in us a more profound conversation with these two powerful patrons for our families.

If you have ever felt alone along your journey to heaven, I urge you to make a retreat of your reading of this book. And see it as a companion for your path. Whether your prayers are on behalf of a spouse in need of God's light, a child who's gone "off the rails," or even for your own need for conversion, you will find here support, understanding, hope, and friends for the journey.

St. Monica, pray for us! St. Augustine, pray for us!

Lisa M. Hendey is the founder and editor of CatholicMom.com and the author of *A Book of Saints for Catholic Moms*. An active speaker, blogger, and writer, Lisa resides in the Diocese of Fresno with her family.

What Would Monica Do?

Surely every parent holds the thought for at least a fleeting moment. It usually comes in that sleep-deprived first year, when the child suddenly, spontaneously does something that looks almost athletic or says something that seems downright poetic. And the love-addled parent thinks, "My child is surely one of the five or six most gifted human beings ever to walk the face of this earth." The imagination opens up vistas of greatness: Nobel Prize-winning novelist, cancer-curing doctor, Major League MVP ballplayer, lawyer arguing a landmark case before the Supreme Court.

Surely such a thought occurred to young Monica as she watched her firstborn, Augustine, toddle about their home in Thagaste, North Africa, in the middle of the fourth century.

For Monica, however, the thought proved true. Her son grew to influence the course of history as very few intellectuals have. As the Roman Empire crumbled, he gave the West a new way to think about civilization. In books such as his *City of God*, he laid the foundations for the social order of the Middle Ages. He is probably the single most influential Christian

13

theologian aside from the authors of the New Testament. No author is cited more often in the *Catechism of the Catholic Church*; no theologian is cited more by St. Thomas Aquinas. Augustine established a baseline for systematic theology in the West. Along the way, he also contributed enormously to other literary genres: the memoir, for example. He wrote hundreds of works, most of which have survived to our own day.

Augustine was the ultimate "gifted child." Yet, he also stands as the very image of a wayward child. He is the adult son who broke his mother's heart — repeatedly, over seventeen years! — and consistently chose a path at odds with his upbringing.

It's a story as old as the world. It's a natural thing for children to separate from their parents. That natural parting is, in many cases, a benign though challenging matter.

Sometimes, though, it's more than challenging. In our damaged world, where all nature suffers the effects of a primeval fall, natural events can be painful and even prone to catastrophe. Children push hard to break free. Sometimes, they rebel. Sometimes, they pursue their rebellion by sinning and even committing themselves to a sinful lifestyle.

Since separation is a normal part of growing up, and since we all limp along with a nature affected by Original Sin, many of us, in the course of a lifetime, find ourselves playing the role of Monica or Augustine — or both roles in succession.

This book is written by two men (blood kin, uncle and nephew) who are young enough to hold vivid memories of our own years of pushing away. We now find ourselves parents to children who must, in their turn, push away and make their own choices. So we find ourselves reflecting often upon the saint who, more than any other, has taught Christians how to parent their adult children. We're growing close to St. Monica.

Looking to St. Monica, though, we can't help but recognize patterns from our own past. We both were raised by women who were prodigies of motherhood. (This is not to slight our fathers, who will require a book all their own.) And so, we conceived the project of considering St. Monica's choices as a parent in light of the modern circumstances we've experienced. What would Monica do, given the sort of children we were — and the sort of children we're now raising? These are not academic questions for us. They're urgent prayers.

The book begins with a biographical sketch of Monica and her famous son, and then proceeds to a series of prayerful reflections on the patterns in their relationship with one another and their relationship with God. We present the book in eighteen chapters — a sort of double novena — to symbolize Monica's extraordinary patience. We want a piece of that action, that patience. This is the most effective way we could think to acquire it.

Each chapter includes our reflection, followed by a meditation taken from the writings of St. Augustine. Then, you will find a brief, practical resolution; and a prayer adapted from the Church's liturgy or from the works of St. Augustine himself.

The saints live in Christ, and they share his intercessory power. Jesus, the "one mediator between God and men" (1 Timothy 2:5), has chosen to make the saints his "fellow workers" (1 Corinthians 3:9). The saints surround us as "so great a cloud of witnesses"

(Hebrews 12:1), ready to share encouragement, wisdom, and consolation.

Before we pray with them, however, it's good to get to know them. That is the subject of our next chapter: the very dramatic story of a mother and her adult son.

Introduction

Monica: Tough Love and the Making of a Saint

She had done nothing to deserve such treatment.

Monica had raised her son well and given him everything in spite of the family's limited means. She and her husband had made sacrifices so that Augustine could get the best education available. They had supported their son materially as he started out on his career.

And this is how he repaid her?

He lied to her.

He dropped her off at a chapel to pray, promising to pick her up in time for their sea voyage to Rome.

And then he abandoned her there — in a port city, miles from her home.

Augustine fled with his mistress and Monica's grandson to a foreign land, without saying so much as goodbye.

In those days of very limited travel, it was quite possible that Monica would never see her son again.

Yet, he had excised her from his life as casually as he might trim off his beard.

She must have been a sight, as she stood at the dock and realized what he had done to her. Many years later, he would confess the matter and report that she wailed aloud. She was angry — angry with herself, for her apparent failure in child rearing. She was angry with God, too, because of his apparent failure to answer her prayers on her timetable. Didn't he see that she wanted only good things? She wanted her son to live like a Christian. She wanted to be part of her grandson's life, to provide a Christian influence for him.

Her best intentions should have been apparent to everyone: to God and to her good-for-nothing son, Augustine. But nobody — or so it seemed that day at the docks in North Africa — nobody was giving her what she was due.

• • • • • • •

Monica was born in A.D. 331 or 332 in Thagaste, a town in North Africa located in modern-day Algeria. She came from a family of modest means. Her family employed servants, but that was normal for "middle class" families at that time. Augustine described his family as poor. The definitions of rich and poor were quite different than they are now. Scholars suggest that Monica's family probably owned a small amount of land. They couldn't be counted among the destitute or slaves, but they weren't affluent either.

North Africa had been part of the Roman world since the middle of the second century before Christ. In 146 B.C., Roman forces destroyed the city of Carthage and then re-established it as a Roman city. Its fertile farmlands made it a valuable part of the Roman world.

The dominant culture in the cities was Latin and Roman, but the people in the towns and rural areas held fast to their ancient Berber identity.

At the time Monica was born, Christianity was newly legal in the Roman Empire. Tolerance had come with Constantine's Edict of Milan in A.D. 313. But Christianity had been present in North Africa for centuries, and it was a distinctive and tough strain of the faith. It appears first in history's paper trail in the mid-100s, with the trial transcripts of martyrs. By the end of the second century, the Church was already well-enough established to boast a vibrant Christian culture.

As the second century gave way to the third, the most important and lasting Christian Latin voices came from North Africa: the fiery lawyer Tertullian, who gave the West its theological vocabulary; the martyr St. Perpetua, who left us her prison journal; and the bishop St. Cyprian, whose writings remain important monuments of Christian doctrine and practice. North African Christianity was known for its passion, its toughness, and its rigor. It was a land of deep learning and defiant martyrs.

In the last great persecution, that of Diocletian at the beginning of the fourth century, the African Church, like all the churches, was struggling with the problem of how to deal with Christians who had committed apostasy. These were Christians who had renounced the faith under pressure, but later regretted their failure. Should they be re-admitted to the sacraments immediately upon repentance? Should they have to undergo some period of public penance? Or, should they be allowed to return only on their death-beds? These were urgent and important questions as some of the *traditores* — "traitors," who had handed over holy books and sacred vessels — were clergymen.

A group called the Donatists (named after a bishop, Donatus) wanted to take a hard line. They said that the sacraments were invalid and ineffective if celebrated by a sinful priest. They expelled from their clergy and congregations anyone who had committed mortal sin. In doing this, they separated themselves from the mainstream of Christian tradition, which tended toward mercy (if sometimes a severe mercy). It soon became clear that Donatism was incompatible with Catholic doctrine and life and, because the two could not coexist, there were mutual excommunications.

Monica grew up in a Christian household in the midst of this drama. We don't know what side her family was on. In all his abundant writings, Augustine does not bring up the matter of his family's allegiance in the previous generations. His silence leads some scholars to wonder if maybe Monica's people were Donatists. It's clear, in any event, that they were passionate about the faith, and they were tenacious about its observance.

As a young girl, Monica would have known people who could still remember the great persecutions — people, perhaps, who survived torture for the sake of Christ. These were known as "confessors." The term "martyrs" was reserved for those who had suffered unto death. She lived among Christians who had been tried, who had endured and triumphed. She lived in a land of many martyred saints.

• • • • • •

Monica learned the faith primarily from an elderly maidservant. Her parents placed a lot of trust in this woman. This maidservant had served a similar role for

Monica's father. As nanny to the children over two generations, she had carried Monica's father on her back, and then his children.

From Augustine's account, we get the impression that this maidservant was something of a drill sergeant. She wanted to train Monica and her siblings not to want what they shouldn't have. So she had them practice self-denial even in legitimate wants. She refused to let them drink *anything* between meals, so that they would learn to control their consumption of wine when they got older.

This strategy didn't always work out well. Wine became, for Monica, the forbidden fruit that sorely tempted her. When she was still a young girl, she acquired the dangerous habit of sneaking a cup whenever she had a chance.

We're grateful that Monica chose to share that embarrassing episode with her son, and that Augustine chose to include it in his *Confessions*. How else would we know that Monica was a typical teenager who broke rules and took stupid risks? Monica's drinking came to an abrupt end when a younger servant, who was looking for a chance to humiliate her, caught her in the act and accused her of being a drunk. We can still feel the teenager's shame, over a thousand years later. To her credit, that was the end of Monica's drinking days. Afterward, when she did drink wine as part of a local religious custom, it was watered down and she would sip a single glass over the course of several hours.

• • • • • •

People in every generation feel that life is short. In the fourth century, however, it tended to be far shorter than it is today. People back then could and sometimes did live past a hundred, but many, if not most, died young by today's standards. Medicine was primitive, and there were no effective ways to fight infectious diseases, cancers, or even allergic reactions. Life expectancy was around thirty. Not surprisingly, people tended to marry young. For girls, marriage at age thirteen was not uncommon.

Marriages were usually arranged by the families, for good or ill. Monica's parents, in fact, chose an odd mate for their child. He was much older than she. He was not a Christian. And he seems to have had some genuinely disagreeable traits. Also, Patricius (or Patrick) turned out to be a womanizer with a violent temper.

We know that Patricius didn't live an edifying moral life. But he seems to have been a hardworking man with a strong sense of civic duty. He served in local government, and he tried to negotiate good educational and professional opportunities for his children as they grew older.

Patricius may have had some sympathies for Christianity — and there is no evidence that he practiced the old Roman religion. At any rate, he was a work in progress. But he gradually came to appreciate the wife he had in Monica. She was a woman who possessed the kind of virtue that won respect without demanding it.

Monica had a strong prayer life and, according to Augustine, went to church twice each day. This probably meant that she attended daily Mass and then some other fixed time of prayer. She fasted according to the local customs, took part in the local devotions — such as visiting graves on the anniversaries of family members' deaths — and celebrated the Church's great festival days along with her neighbors.

Hers was not a mechanical piety. Monica's devotion was heartfelt. Her son would recall that she prayed constantly, often with tears.

• • • • • • •

At the beginning of a marriage in fourth-century Africa, the young wife would customarily move in with her husband's family. Under the best circumstances, this would be a challenge. For Monica, it must have been a shock. A young Christian girl raised in a devout home, she now found herself among a pagan family whose values were quite different from her own.

To her in-laws, too, Monica must have seemed strange. The servants in Patricius's home weren't fond of her at first, and they spread rumors about her that upset her mother-in-law. Through quiet perseverance, Monica was able to win over her mother-in-law and, eventually, the servants as well.

It was not a culture that favored women. Society was indifferent to domestic violence — and even adultery, at least when it was pursued by men. These patterns were so entrenched in pagan cultures that some people looked upon them simply as human nature. Monica knew them to be signs of fallen human nature. She developed techniques to deal with her husband. She would never confront him when he was angry. Nor, however, would she fail to speak up. She would wait until he was calm and then make her point.

Her friends attested to her effectiveness. Even though Patricius was prone to violence, Monica never bore any marks that he had hurt her. On the other hand, some of her friends who were married to less violent men often showed signs of abuse. It sounds shocking by modern standards, but Monica was very tough on her friends in this regard. She told them not just to fall back on blaming their husbands, but to look for ways they could improve themselves and their marriages.

She could say these difficult things because she was a good friend. Neighbors went to her often for advice, and she gained a reputation for solomonic wisdom in helping friends settle disputes and reconcile with one another. People trusted her; they could tell her anything. She never gossiped *to* them, so they knew she would never gossip *about* them.

• • • • • • •

Monica was twenty-three when she gave birth to her first child, Augustine. Eventually she had at least two other children, a son named Navigius — who appears often in Augustine's writings — and a daughter, who also is mentioned by Augustine, though not by name. Some biographies tell us the daughter's name was Perpetua, a common name among North African Christians. Both of Augustine's siblings were devout Christians. We don't have any indications that they went through the sort of rebellious phase that Augustine did.

Monica's firstborn was a precocious child, and his parents recognized his talents early. Patricius found educational opportunities that were beyond the family's means, but he also found a benefactor who recognized Augustine's gifts and helped to foot the tuition bills. Monica was confident that education would strengthen her son's faith.

Augustine was brought up as a Christian, though he was not baptized. At the time, some Christians believed that there could be no forgiveness for serious sins committed after baptism. Because of this, many people chose to delay baptism — often until they believed death was imminent — rather than risk a post-baptismal fall. Many of the saints of this era — Basil the Great, Jerome, and Ambrose, for example — were raised in Christian families, but did not receive baptism till adulthood. Years later, as a bishop, Augustine would speak out forcefully against the practice of delaying baptism. It is the grace of the sacrament, he argued, that gives us the strength to avoid serious sin.

Once, when he was a teenager, Augustine got terribly sick, and his parents thought he was going to die. So his mother began to prepare for his baptism. But he recovered quickly, and the plans to baptize him were put aside.

The years of higher education in the fourth century roughly correspond to the college years today. Recognized as a prodigy, Augustine went off to the big city, Carthage, for his studies. It was a great world capital, a commercial center, a prosperous and bustling metropolis. As the ships and merchants brought spices and carpets and silks from faraway lands, so they also brought ideas. New religious currents arrived from the Orient and became quite trendy, not only in Carthage, but in all the cities of the Roman world. Then, as now, faddish cults gravitated toward the college campuses.

The newest and most sophisticated of the Eastern religions was that of Mani, called Manichaeism. It was a hodgepodge, fusing elements of several major religions: Christianity, Buddhism, Zoroastrianism, Judaism, and Hinduism. Mani proclaimed himself to be the "last prophet" in the line of the religious founders. He died in Persia in A.D. 276, and his religion spread rapidly along the trade routes.

What did the Manicheans believe? They held that there are two coeternal principles — two "gods," if you will. One is good, and the other evil. One is light; the other darkness. In a great cosmic struggle, evil created matter in order to trap elements of the spiritual light. Human beings are spirits of light trapped in the prison of gross material bodies. The prophets, and pre-eminently Mani, came to show the elect the way to liberation. Manicheans held a dim view of everything having to do with the human body, especially sex and reproduction. Making babies just made more prisons for the entrapment of light.

Those who seriously followed Mani were known as the Elect, and they cut an impressive figure in their city neighborhoods. They observed strict celibacy, of course. They strained their water so that they would not accidentally swallow a bug. They were fruitarians, because to eat a vegetable a plant must be destroyed. The Elect, wishing never to harm even a plant, consumed only fruits and nuts, which the trees and shrubs provide abundantly. And they studied esoteric scriptures, applying them to real-life conundrums: If God is good, why is there evil? If God loves us, why do we suffer?

The Manicheans impressed Augustine because they were serious, philosophically inclined, and they promised answers to the thorniest questions of human existence. "Promised" is the key word here. He himself would eventually reject the followers of Mani because they consistently failed to deliver on that promise. When he probed at their pat answers, they would send him on to teachers higher up the chain. Those teachers consistently disappointed him.

But disillusion was still a long time off. In the beginning, the Manichean discipline intrigued Augustine. It was a contrast to his own seriously undisciplined life. Living away from home for the first time, he was sleeping around and partying, although ultimately he settled down with just one woman, and soon got her pregnant. He remained at the periphery of Mani's religion, not as one of the Elect, but as a Hearer, an inquirer.

His academic studies continued apace and he was, without much competition, the hottest academic property in Carthage. When he returned home to Thagaste, Augustine had a girlfriend, a son, a heresy problem, and an ego the size of Africa.

Meanwhile, Monica was trying to run a Christian household. She had recently experienced the joy of her husband's conversion followed, roughly a year later, by the desolation of his death. She still had young and impressionable children at home.

The girlfriend and the grandson Monica could deal with. It was the heresy and the ego that led her to throw Augustine out of the house. Maybe she threw him out in order to bring him to his senses. Or, maybe she did it to protect her other kids from the taint of Manichaeism. Either way, it didn't seem to change anything inside Augustine.

One night, Monica dreamed that Augustine would come back to the faith. She took it as a good omen, and so she allowed him to move back in. When Monica explained the dream to Augustine, he told her that she was the one who was going to convert to his side.

As she had done with her husband, Monica probably developed some techniques for dealing with her know-it-all son. She prevented him from poisoning the minds of the rest of the household. We do know that she sought advice from a bishop who had been raised by Manicheans. This bishop refused to speak to Augustine because he found him vain and proud, and unwilling to listen.

That didn't satisfy Monica. So she continued to bug the bishop until, in exasperation, he told her that a child of so many tears would not be lost. Perhaps he just wanted to get rid of her. But Monica took the bishop's words as a prophecy and continued with renewed strength in her hope that Augustine would come to the truth. It's possible, too, that during the course of their exchange, the bishop explained some things about Manichaeism. Even if Monica wasn't able to convince Augustine of his errors, perhaps she was able to inoculate the rest of her household against them.

And she apparently did. She taught the faith to Augustine's son and live-in girlfriend. We don't know the name of Augustine's companion. It's likely she was still alive when he wrote his memoir, and he granted her the favor of anonymity. The boy's name was Adeodatus, which means "gift of God."

To his credit, Augustine stayed with the same woman for seventeen years. Why didn't they marry? Early in life, Monica and Patricius discouraged Augustine from marriage because they thought it would interfere with his career. It's also possible that he didn't marry his mistress because the law prohibited such a union. If they were from different social classes, there could be no marriage under existing Roman law.

• • • • • • •

Monica kept to her duties. She held the household to-gether while waiting in confident hope for Augustine to come to his senses and return to the Catholic faith. She was also hoping his career would take off, though he was already experiencing his share of professional dis-appointments. His students behaved like thugs. They disrupted class and were not interested in learning.

Someone told him that the grass was greener on the other side of the Mediterranean — that students in Rome were more studious, earnest, decorous, and well-behaved. Based on this urban legend, Augustine decided that Rome was where he wanted to teach.

Monica didn't like the idea, and we can certainly sympathize. If Carthage was a simmering pot of strange religious notions, Rome could only be worse. Going off to Rome, Augustine was possibly moving further from the truth. Moreover, he was taking her grandson away, and that thought could only have pained her.

But Augustine went ahead with his plans, and she accompanied him to the port city. She begged him not to go — just as she had relentlessly begged that bishop to talk with him — until finally he agreed to stay in Africa. Monica didn't believe him, although he seemed sincere enough when, one quiet night when the winds were unfavorable and no ships could leave, he took her to a chapel dedicated to St. Cyprian so she could pray.

As she was praying, the wind changed, and Au-gustine boarded a ship and sailed for Rome. (The jerk.)

Monica was beside herself. How could he have done this? And how could God have ignored her prayers — allowing her son to get away at the very mo-ment she was beseeching heaven to stop him? It must have been tempting for Monica in her pain to write the child off and build a new life without Augustine, hoping the other children (now grown) would do better.

Maybe it crossed her mind, but she didn't go that way. Instead she got on a boat herself and sailed to Rome after her wayward son.

We must not allow ourselves to imagine this in terms of modern travel. Sea voyages in the ancient world were nasty. There were no passenger ships, so you and your fellow travelers got whatever space was left on the merchant vessel after all the pickled fish had been loaded. You felt every wave along the way. There was no refrigeration — the food was iffy. And if a crew member picked up a disease from a stowaway rat, there was really no way to quarantine anyone. On top of all that were dangers from pirates and storms.

Monica's trip to Rome was in fact so stormy that even the seasoned crew was frightened. She comforted them and told them that everything would be O.K. The woman had unconquerable faith. She was confident that she would see her son again and that he would be Catholic.

• • • • • • •

Augustine, in Rome, was enduring his own storms.

His friend had been right. The students were better behaved and smarter, but when it came time to pay their tuition bills at the end of the semester, they would bolt. Augustine was near the top of his profession, but he was almost broke. Worse, he came down with a deadly illness, and the end seemed to be near, just as when he was a teenager. He survived, though, and was offered the Chair of Rhetoric in Milan.

In Augustine's field, that was probably the most prestigious place to land. Milan was the administrative capital of the Western empire. The emperor lived there, with all his court, which meant the best and brightest in the world: poets, philosophers, generals, orators, and diplomats. Of course Augustine took the job, which meant that when Monica got to Rome, he wasn't there. There were no cell phones, there weren't even telegraphs. You can imagine her anxiety — alone in a foreign country.

She asked around and found out that Augustine had moved to Milan. It's worthwhile to pause for a minute to consider how Monica was able get such information. Sociologists today use the term "social capital" to describe the value of interpersonal networks. Monica had social capital, and it's quite likely that it came from her membership in the Church. Because the Church is catholic — that is, universal — she could count on African priests and bishops being in Rome. They would be her likely place to begin an investigation. We do know that, upon her arrival in Milan, she immediately established contact and deep rapport with the bishop there, the great St. Ambrose.

It's strange that Augustine never mentions his surprise when one day Monica suddenly appeared in Milan. Did someone tip him off that she was coming? Did she send word that she was on her way?

What did surprise him, however, was her minimal reaction when he informed her that he was no longer a Manichean. She was pleased, but she kept her eye on the goal, telling him she expected him to be a Catholic before she died. Then she doubled down on her prayer life by going to church often and listening to the sermons of Ambrose.

Monica sensed that Ambrose was the one who could bring Augustine back, and indeed it was his sermons that challenged Augustine's Manichean beliefs and led him to wonder whether he could ever know anything at all. He took up a serious study of the philosophy of Plato — what we today refer to as Neo-Platonism — engaging in discussion with Milan's leading Neo-Platonists, some of whom were Christians.

• • • • • • •

In Milan, Monica adjusted to a new culture — and faced serious questions of Christian practice. Should she fast on Saturday the way the faithful did in Africa — or eat on Saturday as they did in Milan? Augustine asked Ambrose what his mother should do. Ambrose said that when he was in Milan he didn't fast, but when he was in Rome he did, so as not to scandalize or be scandalized. He advised Monica to follow the local customs. (This is where we get the saying, "When in Rome do as the Romans do.")

African Christians also had a custom of bringing food and wine to the tombs of the saints and martyrs, probably a Christian adaptation of a pagan practice. The Christians distributed the food and drink to everyone, but mainly to the poor. With wine involved, however, the practice sometimes degenerated, and folks got drunk — think green beer on St. Patrick's Day. Ambrose prohibited the practice in Milan, and Monica complied immediately.

It's clear that Monica had a life. She was concerned about Augustine, but not obsessed, as some people today portray her, and in fact there was plenty to occupy her attention. Parish life did get interesting in Milan. It was a transitional time. The heir to the throne, Valentinian II, was a boy, and his mother, Justina, was his caretaker. Justina followed a heresy called Arianism, and she decided that the city's basilica should belong to a bishop of her sect. Ambrose, however, was unwilling to give it up, so he locked himself inside with a large number of the faithful, intent on keeping their church or dying as martyrs. Monica was there with him.

Armed imperial guards surrounded the basilica while Ambrose, inside, preached and led the faithful in song to keep their spirits up. Ambrose had a knack for composing memorable songs, and the people sang with gusto. (Monica would take pleasure in singing Ambrosian hymns for the rest of her life.)

Eventually, Ambrose won the staring contest, and the Empress Justina gave up. Monica was once again confirmed in her faith in the power of prayer.

• • • • • • •

Augustine was hovering close to Christianity. Monica saw that. But he couldn't receive baptism as long as he had a mistress, and, as we have seen, there seems to have been some obstacle to his marrying her, such as the possibility that she was from a different social class. For whatever reason, Augustine could not marry the mother of his son, and Monica set out to find a wife for him. They sent his mistress, his companion of seventeen years, back to Africa, where she entered a convent, pledging never to love another man.

Monica soon succeeded in her quest, choosing a girl from a respected family and gaining consent from the girl's parents. She was young, however, and Augustine would have had to wait two years for the marriage to take place. Showing how far he still stood from conversion, he took up with another mistress and continued in his tormented path to faith.

In his mind and in his flesh he felt nothing but conflict, particularly in regard to sex. "When I gave in to lust, habit was born," he said in his *Confessions*, "and when I did not resist the habit it became a necessity." He knew what he must do, but he couldn't bring himself to do it. Living with several friends, they talked philosophy, but this brought him no consolation. He reached no closure.

Reaching the limit of his endurance, Augustine one day threw himself down under a fig tree and implored God, in tears, to give him some answers. From nearby he heard a child's voice saying, *tolle, lege, tolle, lege* — "take up and read, take up and read."

Unable to recall any children's games or songs that had those words, he couldn't help but think it was a divine command. He went inside, snatched up the Bible, opened it at random, and read the first passage his eye fell on: "Let us conduct ourselves becomingly as in the day, not in reveling and drunkenness, not in debauchery and licentiousness, not in quarreling and jealousy. But put on the Lord Jesus Christ, and make no provision for the flesh, to gratify its desires" (Romans 13:13–14). Augustine's conversion was complete.

He related all this to his friend Alypius, who was nearby. Alypius, eager for his own message, took up the text and read the next line: "As for the man who is weak in faith, welcome him" (Romans 14:1). Alypius took this to mean the Church would welcome him, as well.

Quickly, Augustine reported the news to Monica who was, naturally, overjoyed and praised God for granting her even more than she had asked. Augustine no longer desired a wife or worldly ambition, but only salvation.

Augustine finished teaching his courses and then left Milan for the nearby countryside, where he and his friends, his brother, and his son Adeodatus (now a young man of seventeen) would begin to prepare for baptism. Monica lived with them, mothered them, and took part in their lofty conversations, often getting in the last word! Augustine recorded these exchanges in his dialogues, *The Happy Life* and *On Order*.

Monica probably had what's called "household literacy." She could make a grocery list and could read the signs in the market, but it's unlikely that she could read well enough to study the Scriptures. One of the reasons she went to church twice daily was that it afforded her two chances to hear the Word proclaimed and homilies preached. Yet such attentive listening, refined by prayer, gave her a keen mind, and she proved her mettle among the philosophers in the countryside. She also reminded them, now and then, to take breaks from talking and eat their meals.

• • • • • • •

Augustine doesn't give us any details about his baptism, although the group probably returned to Milan for the start of Lent so that they could begin formal instruction. Ambrose would have baptized them during the Easter Vigil, probably at the basilica where the Christians had waited out the imperial troops.

"Free from anxiety" over his past life, as Augustine said, and with his mother's tears finally vindicated, he, his family, and friends decided to return together to Africa and create a cloistered community for prayer and study. They would book passage on a ship out of Rome's port city, Ostia on the Tiber.

When they arrived in Ostia, Monica and Augustine found themselves, one day, with time to talk. As they leaned in a window overlooking a garden at the house where they were staying, Monica told Augustine that there was nothing left that she desired in life, nor was there anything left for her to do. She was satisfied, now that he was home in the Church. They talked about heaven as they stood there, and for a minute it seemed they could contemplate it in ecstasy. Then they fell back to earth.

Soon after, Monica came down with a fever and took to her bed. When she fainted a few days later, Augustine and his brother hurried to her side and were there when she regained consciousness. Monica had always said that she wanted to be buried next to her husband back in Africa, but now she looked intently at her sons and told them that they should bury her in Italy. Augustine remained silent, trying to hold back his tears, but his brother protested and said that for her sake, he hoped she would not die in a foreign country, but at home.

You can hear the maternal affection in her voice when she turned to Augustine and said, "See how he speaks!" She then told them that it didn't matter where they buried her — they shouldn't worry about that. "This only I ask," she said, "that you will remember me at the Lord's altar, wherever you may be."

Monica died peacefully a few days later. She was fifty-six years old.

Augustine, devastated, closed her eyes, and for the remainder of the day he fought to contain his emotions.

That night, alone, he broke down and wept freely, making of his tears, he said, "a pillow for my heart."

Augustine remained in Italy for another year before going on to Africa.

• • • • • • •

Devotion to Monica began soon afterward. We can bet it began with Augustine himself. In his book *On the Care of the Dead* he recalled his mother fondly and said: "If the souls of the dead took part in the affairs of the living, and they themselves were speaking to us in our dreams ... my pious mother would be visiting me every night." Monica, he recalled, had "followed me by land and sea that she might live with me." Even the happiness of heaven could not distract her from loving and consoling "the son whom she loved so deeply, whom she never wished to see sorrowing." It's a funny image — but believable: Monica continuing to pursue her son in death as she had in life.

A mother's love does not end at the grave. If a mother has been faithful, Augustine knew, she could intercede for her children before the Almighty, and in death her prayers would be even more powerful than they were in life. We have already seen what Monica accomplished in her years on earth. She is able to accomplish so much more from heaven.

One of Augustine's wealthy friends put up an epitaph in Ostia as a tribute to her, acclaiming her "a second light" to Augustine's merits. "Mother of Virtues," the epitaph reads, "happy because of [your] offspring ... the glory that crowns you both is greater than the praise of your accomplishments."

In time, Monica's remains were moved to a crypt in the Church of Santa Aurea in Ostia. She shared that resting place with three popes (Linus, Felix, and Anterus) and two other saints (Aurea and Constantia).

In 1162, a French priest living under the Augustinian rule claimed that Monica's remains had been transferred to his monastery in Arrouaise, France. This has never been confirmed, but 1162 was also the year that — as far as we can tell — Monica's feast day began to be celebrated. The date chosen was May 4, the eve of Augustine's conversion. In the late twentieth century, her feast was changed to August 27 — the vigil of the August 28 Memorial of St. Augustine, her son.

In 1430, Pope Martin V requested that Monica's remains be found and then transferred to Rome. Her remains were located at St. Aurea and moved in a wooden box to Rome. The news of this transfer spread, and a crowd began to gather. Numerous miracles were attributed to Monica during this trip, and her remains were transferred to a marble coffin that was temporarily kept at San Trifone before being moved to Rome's Church of St. Augustine, where they reside today.

More than four hundred years ago, St. Francis de Sales encouraged the laypeople whom he saw for spiritual direction to read about Monica in the *Confessions*. She was, for him, a model of holiness in ordinary life.

For good measure, one of the women who saw De Sales for spiritual direction was St. Jane Frances de Chantal (1572–1641). St. Francis wrote to her, "Find the *Confessions* of St. Augustine and read carefully Book VIII and what follows. There you will see St. Monica, a widow like yourself, and her care for her son, Augustine; you will find other things too that will encourage you."

In the mid-1800s in France, the Archconfraternity of Christian Mothers was founded under the patronage of St. Monica and began to spread around the world. In 1881, the organization was launched in the United States at St. Augustine Church in Pittsburgh, Pennsylvania (roughly ten miles from where the authors are working on this book), and from there the Christian Mothers have spread throughout the country.

There can be no doubt that Monica continues the work she began as a young mother. As she consoled and counseled her neighbors in Thagaste, so she intercedes for so many today. She prays with pleading parents, who are birthing their children again by their tears.

"With us was my mother," said St. Augustine in one of his dialogues. "To her merits I owe all that I am."

She is with us, too, and more effective in prayer than she was back then.

Chapter 1

Do Prayers Go Unanswered?

The matriarch of our family, "Nan," was mother to seven (including one of this book's authors) and grandmother to eighteen (including the other author). She was a full-time mother, which for her meant that she prayed without ceasing. When she was cleaning the house, she had a duster in one hand and a Rosary in the other. When she was cooking — and, as a Sicilian, she was always cooking — she was praying her St. Thérèse novena, which she knew by heart.

By 2011, however, it had been almost a decade since she was able to cook or clean. After a stroke in 2001, she was partially paralyzed and confined to a wheelchair and bed. Yet, interiorly, little had changed. So deep were the neural pathways she'd burned through a lifetime of prayerful mothering that she still knew what to do. She prayed. Sometimes, when she was alone in her room, her children passing by would hear her praying out loud, conversationally, as if the object of her prayer (Jesus? Mary? St. Thérèse?) were sitting beside her bed. She was praying, of course, for her children.

That's what she did for a living. It's what she had always done. It's what parents do.

It's what St. Monica did. She begged God to bring her son back from heresy and superstition, back to the practice of the Catholic faith. For the near term, she asked God to keep him from traveling to Rome.

She prayed with groaning and weeping. She channeled her passionate emotion not into anger toward her son or a carefully crafted guilt trip, but rather into prayer. Augustine testified that her tears "watered the earth under her eyes in every place where she prayed."

Yet God seemed not to hear her. Augustine continues: "And what was it, O Lord, that she, with such an abundance of tears, was asking of you, but that you would not permit me to sail? But you ... did not grant what she asked."

Most of us are not so strong, and we're inclined to stop praying when our prayers don't have the effect we desire — when we don't get what we want.

After all, didn't Jesus say: "Ask, and it will be given you; seek, and you will find; knock, and it will be opened to you" (Matthew 7:7)? So why did Monica ask and seek and knock for seventeen years without getting what she wanted? "For everyone who asks receives, and he who seeks finds, and to him who knocks it will be opened" (Matthew 7:8). What's up with that?

Of course, Jesus never specified exactly *what* would be given to us when we ask. We always assume (or wish) it's the thing we want, on exactly the terms we're asking. Indeed, Monica was asking for a good thing — her son's conversion, *right now, without delay.*

As parents, we know that small children often ask for things that are good in themselves, but would be disastrous in a child's life. Children and teens may implore their parents for hunting rifles, automobiles, or exotic pets — good things, but things for which their parents know they're not ready — and the parents have to say, "Not yet."

God is our Father, and sometimes he looks at our best intentions and knows that the time is not yet ripe. Augustine put it this way: God said no to Monica for a while "in order to make me what she was ever asking." And making a reprobate into one of the Church's greatest saints is a process that takes time. God had long since blessed Monica's prayers, but he was working with a better time line.

Monica's prayers changed Monica every bit as much as they changed Augustine. They made her every bit the saint he became. They purified her of selfishness. They taught her patience. She learned to trust God. And she enjoyed many side benefits as well: as she sought advice, she underwent spiritual direction from some of the most remarkable Christians alive in her day.

At age ninety-four, our Nan could not always distinguish between her silent prayers and her spoken prayers. Only then did we have the privilege of hearing her interior life. We can be sure, however, that through long years of mothering and grandmothering, she did not always, and maybe not often, get what she wanted for her children. But we can be sure she got what God wanted; and she learned patient obedience through what she suffered (see Hebrews 5:8).

Meditation

From St. Augustine

"Wait for the LORD; be strong, and let your heart take courage; yea, wait for the LORD!" (Psalm 27:14). But when shall this be? It's hard for a mortal. It's slow for one who loves. But listen to the voice that never deceives, of him who says, "Wait for the LORD." Endure the burning of the reins bravely, and the burning of the heart valiantly.

Think not that what you do not receive has been denied. So that you do not give in to despair, see how it is said: Wait for the Lord.

— Exposition on Psalm 27

Resolution

I will pray for the grace to trust my Father God as I wish my children to trust me.

Prayer

From the eternal home where you are now happy with the son who owes you his life both earthly and heavenly, cast a loving look, O Monica, on the many Christian parents who are now fulfilling on earth the hard but noble mission that was once yours. Their children are also dead with the death of sin; and they would restore them to true life by the power of their parental love. After the Mother of Jesus, it is to you that they turn, O Monica, whose prayers and tears were once so fruitful. Take their cause in hand. Maintain their courage; teach them to hope.

Chapter 2

The Meal

For as long as anyone can remember, Nan served Sunday dinner at noon. She expected all seven of her children and numerous grandchildren to be there — even those who lived an hour and a half away.

If anyone was missing, she would say, "Nobody's here!" — much to the chagrin of those who were there. Of course as her children got older and had their own families, the days when "Nobody's here" became more numerous.

Regardless, she always cooked as if the whole family might show up as well as a few cousins and any other unannounced guests. The event had certain rules, which were ironclad, though unstated.

- You didn't have to call ahead to say if you were coming.

- You had to eat until you were ready to pass out.

- You had to take some leftovers with you when you left.

If you didn't follow the rules, Nan would keep after you until you provided the answer she was looking for.

Looking back, it's hard for us to imagine how she cooked for twenty-five people (more or less) once a week for sixty years. Didn't she get tired? Didn't she ever want to do something else for a change? We could never do what she did because we have so many other things going on.

For Nan, it wasn't a task. It was an extension of her. You could even say that it was an extension of the Mass that she attended that morning. She was Martha and Mary rolled into one. Jesus said to Martha, "You are anxious and worried about many things. There is need of only one thing. Mary has chosen the better part and it will not be taken from her" (Luke 10:41–42, NAB).

Nan was not troubled about the many things. She wasn't even troubled about getting the meal together. For her, feeding others was the best part. It was *the* part.

St. Monica, another Mediterranean mother, showed love through food. We see this when she is staying with her son and his companions in Cassiciacum — the country estate near Milan where Augustine and his friends lived while they prepared for baptism. Theirs was no ordinary parish RCIA group. Augustine recorded the dialogues they had, and they were worthy of Plato.

In his dialogue titled *Against the Academics*, the young friends are engaged in a long exchange, and Monica interrupts — twice — and tells them to come in and eat some lunch.

Man does not live on talk alone. We need to eat. We prefer to eat in the company of others.

Augustine is a master storyteller, and if he provides such small details, he's doing so deliberately. They're important. He doesn't mention bathroom breaks, though they surely must have been part of the routine. With Monica's persistent reminder, Augustine is trying to draw our attention to a bigger picture.

While he and his friends dither, unbaptized, outside the "house," Mother Church invites them in to her table, and she does so insistently.

The scene works beautifully on two levels, the natural and the supernatural. On the natural level, it reminds us that it's good to spend regular "face time" with the people we love, and that meals somehow make the event even happier. On the supernatural level, Monica's insistent call reminds us of Mother Church's call for us to go to the sacraments — Reconciliation, then Eucharist — and not allow ourselves to remain "outside the house."

Monica's meals, and our own, serve as a sign of a higher truth. And it's an abiding truth. Read the whole Bible and you'll see the same story played out, again and again. So many of the major events of salvation history take place in the context of a meal. Adam and Eve share a piece of fruit. Abraham and Sarah take the time to serve a meal to three angels. The Israelites eat the Passover as they prepare to leave Egypt. So much of Jesus' activity is taken up with meals, banquets, and feasting — at Cana in Galilee, at the homes of Zacchaeus and of Simon the Pharisee and of Lazarus, at the Last Supper, and then again at Emmaus. The Book of Revelation shows the culmination of history to be a family wedding feast, the Marriage Supper of the Lamb.

It is the way of Mother Church and of the home as well. It is an earthly image of one of the deepest mysteries of God.

A mother feeds her child. It may begin with a baby at the breast. Before long it proceeds, perhaps, to "care packages" sent to distant lands.

It is good, though, whenever we can, to take the time and make an effort to break bread together, to look at one another and talk and laugh. When we do, it's more than fun. It's a sign of a family most perfect, a home most permanent, a banquet most lavish, and a Love divine, all loves excelling.

Meditation

From St. Augustine

Beloved, in our neediness and poverty let us grieve for those who seem to themselves to have everything. For their joy is like that of madmen. A madman rejoices for the most part in his madness, and laughs, and grieves over someone who is sane. So let us rejoice, beloved, if we have received the medicine from heaven, because we all were madmen, and we were healed because we do not love the things we once loved.

We should groan to God on behalf of those who are yet in madness, for he is able to save them too. What they need is to look at themselves and be displeased with what they see — to see what they desire — and yet they don't know how to look at themselves. For if they briefly turn their eyes upon themselves, they see their own confusion....

May God who sees to this, see to it; and may his mercy be present to heal all. Let us who have come together feed upon the feast of God, and let our joy be his word. For he has invited us to his gospel, and he is our food. Nothing could be sweeter, for those who have a healthy palate in the heart.

— Tractates on the Gospel of John, 7.2

Resolution

I will try to begin meals by praying Grace. I will try to make all meals an occasion of at least silent prayer and of service in imitation of Christ.

Prayer

You were called the "Mother of the Poor," Monica, because you cared for them in their needs, and in giving to them you gave to Christ. O Mother and Matron, be an advocate and patron for us, your children, and for our children so that when we leave the flesh, we may be united with you and Augustine, your son, in the joys of paradise. Amen.

Chapter 3

Stay Close

"Don't forget: tomorrow's Ascension Thursday. It's a holy day of obligation."

So ended a typical phone conversation between one of the authors of this book and his mother. The reminder's not so unusual — unless you stop to consider that the son was in his thirties and editing one of the largest-circulation Catholic newspapers in the country. Did she think he didn't know?

No. Mom found her ways to stay close and say what needed to be said.

It's not always easy, though, to stay close. As children approach adulthood, they have a natural impulse to push away, to establish a separate life, to be independent, to make their own choices. Often, they'll do things differently from the way their parents did, and it's easy for parents to take each instance of this as a reproach and a rejection. In fact, sometimes it is. Sometimes kids will mark their adulthood by doing something their parents would never do.

Yet we don't have to take everything as an insult — or make a tattoo or piercing the moral equivalent of war.

We can, instead, choose to respect each child's ability to think outside the box … even when the box is one we made for them and furnished with love.

Most of their choices, we hope, will be morally neutral. It's different, of course, when they choose something — or even pursue a lifestyle — that's immoral. Then we mustn't approve their choices or even appear to approve them. But we still need to find a way to stay close.

It's never easy, and there's no one-size-fits-all solution. St. Monica faced the problem repeatedly. At one point, she refused to have Augustine live in her house as long as he adhered to the Manichean heresy. She was not scandalized as much by his living with a mistress and fathering a child out of wedlock; but she saw (rightly) that heresy was the greatest of his problems. Love for his young family could lead him to God; but heresy could only lead him away.

Eventually, she took him back, along with his mistress and child, in hope that she could exercise some influence over him, as she could not when he was staying with friends.

Monica did what she needed to do in order to stay close to her son. When he was offered a job overseas, she made plans to go along with him, even though he preferred that she stay home. When he abandoned her through trickery, she followed him anyway, and arrived in Italy soon after he did.

Remember that, in her day, there were no cell phones or email, and even the postal service was slow and unreliable. Travel, especially by sea, was extremely dangerous. So the only way to stay close was by remaining physically present.

Modern critics have disparaged Monica as a transcontinental stalker. But she wasn't. There was simply no other way for her to keep in touch with her son, no other way to continue to mother him. If she had simply cut him off, let him go, she would have foregone any future influence on his life. She couldn't let herself to do that — even if it was what he preferred. She needed to be at least at the periphery of his life, so that she could help him to find his way beyond his moral messes and onward to Christ.

We, too, need to stay close to our children. Today, we need not go to sea to do so. We have wondrous options for regular communication. We should use them, prayerfully, as a means of encouragement. We should use them to express our love. Our communications need not, and should not, be a constant moral harangue or overtly religious witness. We can accomplish a lot by our simple constancy and our genuine care. We can serve as the fixed point in a turbulent world. We're there to catch them when they're ready to fall.

And every now and then, God will give us an opportunity to speak his name in a way that is helpful and healing.

Meditation

From St. Augustine

I was persuaded to go to Rome, and teach there what I had been teaching at Carthage.... My mother wept grievously over my journey, and went with me as far as the sea. She held on to me, begging me to stay with her or allow her to come with me. But I deceived her, pretending that I had a friend whom I could not leave until he had a favorable wind to set sail.

I lied to my mother — and such a mother! — and got away.... I persuaded her to remain that night in a place quite close to our ship, where there was a chapel in memory of the blessed Cyprian. That night I secretly left.... The wind blew and filled our sails, and withdrew the shore from our sight. She, wild with grief, was there in the morning, and filled Your ears with complaints and groans.... [Yet, in time] my mother, made strong by her piety, came to me, following me over sea and land.

— *Confessions* 5.8.15

Resolution

I will find ways to "stay close" to each of my children.

Prayer

Through Monica's shower of tears, a light shone brightly within the Church. She sowed in weeping, but harvested in joy. O Mother and Matron, be an advocate and patron for us and for our children, so that when we leave this mortal flesh we may together be united with you and to Augustine, your son, in the joys of paradise.

Chapter 4

Today. Now.

In the fourth century, it was the custom in some places to ceremonially dedicate a newborn baby to Christ, but defer baptism till later in life. In his *Confessions* (1.11), Augustine recalled: "Even as a boy I had heard of the eternal life promised to us through the humility of the Lord our God condescending to our pride. I was signed with the Sign of the Cross, and I was seasoned with his salt even from the womb of my mother."

St. Monica knew that parenting begins in earnest "from the womb," if not long before. We will be better parents precisely to the degree that we are better Christians. Thus we should not put off for tomorrow what will benefit us and our children today.

We need to take steps to draw closer to Jesus, and to introduce our children to Jesus. We should be grateful that the Church's universal practice now favors the baptism of infants. Thus, from their earliest days, they may live as God's children as well as our children.

Monica dutifully kept the customs of her ancestors. She observed the ceremonies of the Church. But she did not stop there, and neither should we. We need to give Christian witness to our children, twenty-four hours a day, seven days a week, beginning "from the womb," but continuing throughout our lives as parents. Our sons and daughters need to see, as Augustine saw, that we don't take vacations from our faith — or even short breaks. We never take time off from charity and kindness. We pray often, so that we may learn to "pray always" (1 Thessalonians 5:17).

From our constancy, our children learn God's constancy. It is good for them to see this from their earliest days. But it's never too late for us to begin, or begin again, to live out our Christian calling. We can make up for lost time, with the help of God who transcends time. Monica's story and Augustine's story bear witness to this.

The need is urgent, no matter where we are in our progress as parents. We must grow, as Monica did, in holiness, goodness, Christian discipline, and knowledge of doctrine; and this will be true as long as we are parenting — or even just preparing to be parents. It will be true as long as we are alive, even if we should experience the sorrow of those who outlive their own children. We never stop mothering or fathering our kids. If all we can do, sometimes, is pray for them, then we are left with the *best* thing we can do for them. We will do this better the more we are converted to Christ.

Meditation

From St. Augustine

If you seek and relish the things that are above, you desire things everlasting and sure; and as long as you do not yet possess them, you ought to regard yourself as in dire need, even though all your family are spared to you and live as you wish. If you act this way, surely your example will be followed by your most devout daughter-in-law, and the other holy widows and virgins who are settled in peace under your care; for the more pious the manner in which you keep your house, the more are you bound to persevere fervently in prayer.

— *Letter to Proba* 16.30

Resolution

I will provide my child with one of the finest things in life: a truly Christian parent. For the sake of my child's conversion, I will seek my own conversion, without delay.

Prayer

O God, with You we are not disturbed by those who refuse to believe. Instruct me, show me, give me my provision for the way. If it is by faith that we must find You, then grant faith; if by virtue, grant virtue; if by knowledge, grant knowledge. Increase in me faith, hope, and charity. Amen.

Chapter 5

Tell Him What You Really Think

Augustine was not there in Carthage when his mother discovered he had deceived her and abandoned her — but he had no trouble imagining the scene. He addresses Our Lord in the *Confessions* (5.8.15): "The wind blew and filled our sails, and withdrew the shore from our sight. She, wild with grief, was there in the morning, and filled Your ears with complaints and groans, which You disregarded.... Like all mothers, though even more than others, she loved to have me with her, and didn't know the joy You were preparing for her by my absence."

Monica was not shy about shedding tears when she prayed. She told God what she thought and felt. Nor did she hold back when she was upset with him. When she went down to the docks only to learn that her son had left her, she filled God's infinite ears with complaints and groans.

That's how God Himself taught her to pray. The Church looks to the biblical Book of Psalms as the model prayer book. The Psalms present themselves as prayer; and, being biblical, they are inspired by God. St. Augustine taught his congregations to think of the Psalms as prayers *of* Christ, as prayers *to* Christ, and as prayers *about* Christ.

When we think of the Psalms, we like to imagine King David singing his songs and maybe even dancing along with them, as he did before the Ark of the Covenant: "Rejoice in the LORD, O you righteous!" (Psalm 33:1) … "Make a joyful noise to God, all the earth" (Psalm 66:1).

But rejoicing is hardly the whole picture, for almost half the Psalms in the Psalter are psalms of lament or complaint. They freely express impatience with God's timetable.

"O Lord, how long will you look on?" (35:17, NAB)

"How long, LORD? Will you utterly forget me?" (13:1, NAB)

"How long, LORD? Will you hide forever?" (89:47, NAB)

"O LORD, … how long shall the wicked exult?" (94:3)

Those model prayers, those prayers of Christ, really do teach us how to vent our frustration, bewilderment, and disappointment with the way God answers our prayers. He is our Father. He can take it.

The practice can also help us to sympathize with the frustration of our children when we must deny their requests. We ourselves are learning, as St. Monica did, how difficult it is to trust *even a divine Father* when He tells us, "Trust me."

The practice can help us to be patient as we talk our children through their bewilderment over our long-term plans, or when we ask them to defer some gratification for a little while longer.

We should not deny our children their feelings of frustration, but rather help them to express them respectfully, as we do, when we pray as St. Monica did.

Meditation

From St. Augustine

You are impatient; but what seems a long time coming to you will soon come to pass. It is infirmity that makes our wait seem long when it is really short, as you see in the longings of sick men. Nothing seems so long as the mixing of medicines for someone who needs them. His attendants work speedily so as not to anger him. Yet he cries out: "When will it be done? When will it be mixed? When will it be served?" Those who are waiting on you are making haste, but your sickness makes long what is being done speedily.

So consider our Physician attending to the sickness of the patient who says, "How long shall I have to endure? How long will it be?" ... How long in coming, then, is the moment for which we are impatient, and are saying, "When will it come? Will it tarry long?" This our children will say after us, and our children's children, too; and, though each one of these in succession will say this same thing, still that "little while" that is yet to be passes away, as all that is already past has passed away already! O you sick one! "Yet a little while, and the wicked will be no more; though you look well at his place, he will not be there. But the meek shall possess the land" (Psalm 37:10–11).

— *Exposition on Psalm 37*

Resolution

I will tell God what I think and feel.

Prayer

Grant that I may seek You, O my Father, and save me from error. Save my children from error. Hear the prayers of St. Monica on their behalf. When I seek You, let me not find anything else but You. If there is in me any vain desire, cleanse me and make me fit to look upon You ... that I may dwell in Your most blessed kingdom. Amen.

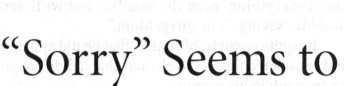

Chapter 6

"Sorry" Seems to Be the Hardest Word

Thanks to the genius of her son, St. Monica's voice rings vividly more than a thousand years after her death. Augustine set down their conversations in loving detail, and so we find ourselves eavesdropping on discussions and debates. We hear the son putting questions to the mother, and the mother answering in ways that show her to be shrewd, passionate, intelligent, devout, and deliberate. We hear a mother admonishing her son.

What we don't find anywhere — and this should be surprising — is an apology. Augustine does wrong by his mother for seventeen years. He disobeys her. He lies to her. He abandons her. He embarrasses her. He says hurtful things to her. Like the Prodigal Son in the Gospel, he spends down the inheritance of faith he had received from his mother.

Then he returns to the Catholic faith and amends his life. It is from that transitional period that he preserved the most conversations with his mother. We can read those conversations from end to end, and we'll find Augustine and Monica talking about everything, even the weather, but we'll never find him saying, "I'm sorry, Mom."

It's quite possible, of course, that he did apologize, and considered the fact so obvious that it didn't require a paragraph in his memoir.

But it's just as possible that he didn't apologize — that he found it too difficult or too awkward — or that his mother made it clear that it was unnecessary, that all was forgiven.

He wrote his *Confessions* when he was still a relatively new Christian, and the book itself represents his early effort to work things out. He makes it clear that he recognized the mistakes of his past and he repented of them before God. But sometimes saying "sorry" to God comes more easily than saying it to a family member.

We can see that Monica must have forgiven her son many times over. But we have no clear evidence that he ever asked for her forgiveness.

We, too, must be prepared to forgive often, because we live in a communion of clumsy saints. We often have some modicum of good intentions, but we're held back by pride. Back in the 1970s (when we were kids), one of the top-rated television series was *Happy Days*. The main character on the show was Fonzie, a superconfident outlier who wore a leather jacket and took meticulous care with his slicked-back hair. He couldn't pass a mirror without admiring himself. In one episode, "The Fonz" made a mistake for which he had to apologize — and all of his organs of speech rebelled against the action. He choked on the phrases "I was wrong" and "I'm sorry." His lips and his tongue fell paralyzed: "I was wrrrrrrrr...."

We viewers laughed at Fonzie's vanity, but none of us kids forgot the scene. Even if we didn't have Fonzie's self-confidence or good looks (and your authors certainly didn't), we still had trouble saying those phrases to our family members.

Augustine had earned his self-confidence even more than Fonzie did, yet he may have encountered the same paralysis.

Or maybe his mother sensed his sorrow, even if he never expressed it, and let him know that apologies were unnecessary.

We should cultivate, for ourselves, the habit of saying "I'm sorry." If we're estranged from someone, they may be waiting to hear those words from us. Even if we don't believe the fault for the estrangement is primarily our own (people rarely do), our apology can help bring relief and closure to the other person. It's a big sacrifice to make, but it's a work of mercy, and it's worth the strain.

We should be demanding of ourselves when we make an apology, avoiding any qualifiers or lawyerly provisos that carry an implication of blame: "I'm sorry, *but* ..." or "I'm sorry, *even though*...."

We should be demanding of ourselves, but merciful with others. Go and reread the Parable of the Prodigal Son. The wayward young man rehearses a lengthy apology (Luke 15:18–19), but his father runs out to meet him and won't even let him finish the memorized speech. He interrupts him halfway. Dad has already moved on to the next, happier phase of their relationship.

Sometimes we hold such anger toward others that we feel a deep *need* to hear an apology. So we ask for one. But then the apology's not good enough. They didn't say the things we wanted them to say, the way we wanted them to be said. When it comes to righting our own grievances, we can become as fussy as a coffee snob who keeps sending back one flawed latte after another.

We cannot make someone else sorry. We can't change others. But with God's grace, we can change ourselves. We can move from grievance to forgiveness, and we can move again and again and again and again — maybe seventy times seven times. We can learn to do this. And we must.

It's quite possible that St. Monica did. It's quite likely that our own parents did.

Learn from God. When we go to confession, he does not demand perfect contrition. He's willing to work with any gesture. There's a scene in Disney's animated feature *Alladin* where the genie wants to save the boy's life, but Alladin is unconscious, so he can't command it. So the genie lifts the boy's head up and lets it fall back down, and says: "I'll take that as a yes."

God is eager to work with whatever little bit of sorrow we show. We should imitate him in our family life.

Meditation

From St. Augustine

You are just at the point of saying to me, "But I'm not God, I'm a human being, a sinner." Thank God that you confess you have sins.

Forgive then, that they may be forgiven you.

The Lord our God exhorts us to imitate Him. God Himself, Christ, exhorts us. Of him the Apostle Peter said: "Christ also suffered for you, leaving you an example, that you should follow in his steps. He committed no sin; no guile was found on his lips" (1 Peter 2:21–22). He truly had no sin, yet he died for our sins, and shed his blood for the forgiveness of sins. He took up for our sakes what was not his due, that he might deliver us from what was due to us. Death was not due to Him, nor life to us. Why? Because we were sinners. Death was not due to Him, nor life to us. He received what was not due to Him. He gave what was not due to us. But since we are speaking of the forgiveness of sins, lest you should think it too high a thing to imitate Christ, listen to the Apostle: "Be kind to one another, tenderhearted, forgiving one another, as God in Christ forgave you. Therefore be imitators of God" (Ephesians 4:32–5:1).

They are the Apostle's words, not mine. Is it indeed a proud thing to imitate God? Listen to the Apostle, "Be imitators of God, as beloved children." You are called a child: if you refuse to imitate Him, why do you seek his inheritance?

I would say this even if you had no sin you wanted forgiveness for. But as it is, whoever you are, you are human. Though you are righteous, you are human. Whether you are a layman or monk, priest or bishop or apostle, you are human.

Listen to the Apostle's voice, "If we say we have no sin, we deceive ourselves" (1 John 1:8)…. He says, "*If*" … He joined himself in the guilt, that he might be joined in the pardon, too. "If we say we have no sin, we deceive ourselves, and the truth is not in us. If we confess our sins, he is faithful and just, and will forgive our sins and cleanse us from all unrighteousness."

How does he cleanse? By forgiving! It's not as if he finds nothing to punish. He has, after all, found something to forgive! So then, if we have sins, let's forgive.... Let's not retain enmities in our heart against another. For the retaining of enmities, more than anything, corrupts this heart of ours.

— *Sermon 64 on the New Testament*

Resolution

I will be quick to forgive, quick to apologize, eager to reconcile.

Prayer

O God, the comforter of the sorrowful and salvation of those who hope in You: You mercifully accepted the pious tears of the blessed Monica in the conversion of her son Augustine. Grant us, by the intercession of both, to deplore our sins and to find the pardon of Your grace. Grant, through their intercession, that our children, too, turn from sin and seek Your grace. Through Christ our Lord.

Chapter 7

The Need
Is Mutual

It happens often enough when we go to Mass. During the homily, the pastor invites an older couple to stand in front of the altar and renew their wedding vows. This time it took off in a surprising direction.

It was their sixtieth wedding anniversary. They had been married in that very church. The priest began to recite all of the couple's accomplishments — an impressive listing, and quite long.

"For fifty-five years, he's been a member of the Holy Name Society," the priest said, adding drama and volume with each line on the resumé. There was such a buildup that there either had to be a climax or the priest was going to lose his voice. "And together they raised these eight wonderful children!"

At that point, the husband broke protocol. He reached over and grabbed the microphone from the priest's hand and said, "Correction, Father, they raised me." And then he handed back the microphone.

It threw the whole idea of parenting upside down for at least some of us in the congregation. Aren't parents supposed to raise their children? It sounded absurd, but at the same time it made perfect sense. It made perfect sense if you looked at it from God's perspective, and his loving plan for the gradual perfection of *all* his children.

Parenting isn't another job to accomplish. It isn't something to check off our to-do list before moving on to the next item. Parenting helps us to become the saint God wants us to be. It was just like the old man said. Our children raise us.

We have a natural desire to please our children and provide for them. We are physically, psychologically, and spiritually hardwired for this. So much of our natural equipment — the sex drive, the process of gestation and birth, the swelling of a mother's breasts — is designed by God to make us givers. We give life. We give growth. We give sustenance. Nature drives us to do so.

Yet we should never forget that we are also on the receiving end of this exchange. Our children give to us even by their taking. Augustine points out that his need, in infancy, to fill his belly answered his mother's need to empty the swell of her breasts.

We are takers as well as givers. If we forget this, we will always feel unappreciated or underappreciated. If we forget this, we will never be humble. For to be humble is to be grateful always, to know that we receive far more than we give, and that we give nothing that we have not first received from God.

If we do not acknowledge what our children do for us, and have done for us, our love will be stunted and our resentment will grow; and nothing poisons a relationship as resentment does.

We should thank God for the gift of our children and the gifts they give us. And we should find occasions, now and then, to thank our children for what they do and who they are and the difference they've made in our lives.

God made us to need one another so that we can effectively love one another. Thus, when we give, we too are the beneficiaries. We are fulfilling our nature. At the same time, we are transcending our nature as we become more Godlike, empowered to give more and more.

"God loves a cheerful giver" (2 Corinthians 9:7). Let us give always with a smile, expecting nothing in return, knowing all that we have received. Our children will learn generosity from our deeds. They will learn gratitude from our gratitude.

Meditation

From St. Augustine

> Though they sustained me by the consolation of woman's milk, neither my mother nor my nurses filled their own breasts. It was You, Lord, through them, who gave me the food of infancy according to Your order and Your bounty, which underlie all things. For it was You who caused me not to want more than You gave, and it was You who gave those who nourished me the will to give me what You gave them. And they, by an instinctive affection, were willing to give me what You had supplied abundantly. It was indeed good for them that my good should come through them — though,

really, it was not from them, but by them. For it is from You, O God, that all good things come.

— *Confessions* 1.6

Resolution

I will learn to say thank you often, in my home and in my prayer.

Prayer

I give thanks to You, Lord of heaven and earth, giving praise to You for my earliest days and infancy.... Even then I had life and being; and as my infancy closed I was already seeking for signs by which my feelings might be made known to others. Where else could such a creature come from, but from You, O Lord? (Prayer of St. Augustine, *Confessions* 1.6.10)

Chapter 8

Blessed Peacemaker

The saddest stories in the Bible — and the stories with the most catastrophic consequences — are those that deal with divided families. Cain is consumed by envy of his brother Abel. Joseph's brothers conspire against him. Absalom goes to war against his father, King David.

Few situations are so heartbreaking to parents as seeing their household break down into factions. Yet the parents can indeed find themselves standing on one side looking across the divide at family members who are estranged from them.

Estrangement is sometimes a fact of life, but we should try never to indulge it as a feeling. We should pray for reconciliation, strive to keep close to God, and know that in God we are close to everyone and everything — even those who screen out our calls and don't return our emails.

Monica was a peacemaker. Augustine referred to this quality as a "great gift" from God. When friends or family members would complain about one another, he recalled, "she would listen to both sides tell the most bitter things — raging and undigested discord giving vent to crude enmity in bitter speeches."

She would let them vent, but she would never repeat the mean things they'd said. She would only repeat "what might lead to a reconciliation."

Augustine contrasts this with the normal human tendency to seek allies or take sides when things begin to break down. While this may bring some temporary feeling of consolation, it is always bad for families or friendships. Augustine decries those who "through some horrible and far-spreading infection of sin, not only disclose to enemies mutually enraged the things said in passion against each other, but even add things that were never said at all."

We should learn from Monica, he says, and be generous. Never take sides. Always be a bridge, not a wall or a weapon. "To a generous person, it ought to seem a small thing not to incite or increase personal enmity by ill-speaking." We should also "extinguish acrimony with kind words."

"That's how she was," Augustine says to Our Lord. "You, her most intimate Instructor, taught her in the school of her heart" (*Confessions* 9.9.21). We, too, should enroll in that school.

We should examine our relationships. If we find that we have arrayed one family member against another, or placed ourselves with one against another, we should repent and do all we can — and let God do all he can in us — to heal the breach.

Meditation

From St. Augustine

> Let strife be banished and peace invited to return, lest this one who is your friend be lost to you, and the devil who is your enemy rejoice over you both.

> — *Letter 250.3*

Resolution

I will not lead family members to speak ill of other family members. Nor will I allow myself to be drawn into such divisions.

Prayer

O Lord, out of many souls there shall be hereafter one city, made up of those who have one soul and one heart toward God. After we have completed our sojourn in a strange land, may the perfection of unity be ours. There, the thoughts of all shall never be hidden from one another, nor in anything be opposed to one another. O Monica, pray for healing of the divisions within our family, especially between parent and child.

Chapter 9

The Big Talks

Some devout friends of ours told us a sad story. Their daughter had been dating someone who was not only a non-Christian but hostile to Christianity. Their daughter had also stopped practicing her faith, and the two were engaged — and planning a wedding ceremony that openly mocked Christianity. The parents were heartbroken; it was too late to say anything now. They left it all in God's hands. After all, the daughter was an adult capable of living her own life. What was to stop her from moving away and rejecting them completely?

The story illustrates that in the relationship between parent and child, there are going to have to be difficult conversations. They can't be delayed forever in the hope that the issues will work themselves out on their own. Also, sometimes when you do have the conversation, it doesn't go well — at least initially.

Monica experienced this with Augustine. When he returned from Madaura, where he had attended "prep" school, Monica learned that Augustine was engaging in sexual activity. Remember that her husband, Patricius, himself was inclined to adultery. The old man was also eager to have grandchildren. You can imagine the pain that it caused Monica. For the sake of Augustine's own soul — and for the sake of the women he casually embraced — she couldn't allow Augustine's sins to go without remark.

Her big talk was carefully calibrated. She knew that preaching piety to a weak believer was probably futile. So she told him plainly that he should be chaste; but if he would not, then he should stay away from married women. She could not stand the thought of her son becoming a homewrecker. If she could not lead him to reform, she would at least (to the best of her abilities) contain the damage he might do.

Years later, Augustine could see God speaking through his mother. It's hard to tell if Monica saw it that way also. We'll assume that she was too humble to imagine herself as the voice of God, but we can probably be certain that she prayed about the conversation long before it took place. We can learn from that and from other aspects of the exchange.

Note that she had the conversation in secret and in private. She didn't embarrass Augustine. She showed respect for his dignity in the sight of others. In fact, we don't get the sense that she told anyone in the household what she was going to say to her son before she said it.

Augustine was only sixteen at the time, but he was probably already so accomplished a speaker that if the conversation were held in front of an audience, he could have turned it into a circus — and made his mother look bad.

We can imagine Monica's anxiety leading up to the conversation. She knew that Augustine would be angry with her. And Augustine himself, years later, admitted to despising Monica when she corrected him on this issue. So it's not as if good preparation and good intentions gained her any great short-term reward. Augustine refused to listen, and he held her in scorn. Even worse, he increased his womanizing after Monica's reproach.

You can imagine Monica's heartbreak and frustration. But Augustine never forgot the conversation. And eventually, more than a decade and a half later, it brought about a change in him that was greater than anything Monica had hoped for. When he gave up the recreational approach to sex, he at first heeded his mother and sought a monogamous relationship in marriage — but God called him to be celibate — and, more, to be a bishop and, most of all, to be a saint.

Meditation
From St. Augustine

We will hear it said, "Let our elders prescribe what we should do, and let them pray for us to do it. But don't let them admonish or correct us if we fail to do it."

No, let all these things be done, since the Apostles, the teachers of the churches, did them all. They prescribed what should be done, and they admonished if things did not get done, and they prayed that everything might be done. The Apostle prescribes when he says: "Let all that you do be done in love" (1 Corinthians 16:14). He admonishes when he says: "To have lawsuits at all with one another is defeat for you. Why not rather suffer wrong? Why not rather be defrauded? But you yourselves wrong and defraud, and that even your own brethren. Do you not know that the unrighteous will not inherit the kingdom of God?" (1 Corinthians 6:7–9). And we also hear him pray: "May the Lord make you increase and abound in love to one another and to all men, as we do to you" (1 Thessalonians 3:12). He prescribes charity to be practiced. He prays that charity may abound.

This is the point: in the elders' precepts, learn what you ought to have; in their admonitions, learn that it is your own fault that you don't have it; in their prayers learn where you may receive what you wish to have.

— Admonition and Grace 3

Resolution

I will be both brave and kind when I need to correct someone.

Prayer

Cast a loving look, O Monica, on the many Christian parents who are now fulfilling on earth the hard but noble mission that was once your own. Their children are also lifeless with the death of sin, and they would restore them to true life by the power of parental love. They turn to you, O Monica, whose prayers and tears were once so effective and fruitful. Take their cause in hand. Maintain their courage. Teach them to hope. Intercede for them before the throne of the Almighty. We ask this, as we ask all things, through Our Lord Jesus Christ. Amen.

Chapter 10

Getting Help

When the kids were grown and dispersed to other states, Nan and Pop regularly packed the car with food and gifts and went off to see their growing grandchildren. Those days were filled with feasting and light conversation.

Once, however, they arrived in the middle of a crisis. Their daughter Susie's son, a freshman in high school, was extremely angry and directing all of his rage toward his parents.

For years he'd wanted a dog, and his dream came true that year. The dog was his constant companion and closest friend. Unfortunately, it had also made a number of enemies — by biting any child who came close enough to him. The neighbors were upset. Training repeatedly failed. Mom and Dad made the hard decision that the dog had to go.

They explained it reasonably and lovingly, but their teen son was hearing none of it. For him the dog was not the problem. His parents were the problem. In his rage, he said many things he'd later regret.

His mom was hurt and frustrated — and hurting for her son. Yet she couldn't get through to him. His rage was a wall.

One Saturday, Nan and Pop arrived, all smiles — just as she arrived at her wit's end. As they entered the house, she unloaded the whole situation onto Pop.

Pop was experienced with teens, having raised seven children through those years. An almost silent man, he was an affectionate grandfather. His grandchildren, in fact, had never heard him raise his voice.

But that particular day, that particular grandson did. Pop led him away a distance and talked tough. Today, as that grandchild writes this book, he remembers the surprising tone and the unprecedented volume, but only a few of the words. "What are you thinking?... your mother ... dog ... lawsuit."

The meeting was brief and successful. Pop and grandson returned. Grandson apologized to mom. The dog would indeed be leaving.

Monica frequently got to her wit's end with her son Augustine and even asked people outside the family to talk to him. She once visited a bishop who had himself been a Manichean. Because of his background, he had been able to convince many people to turn away from the heresy.

Naturally, Monica sought him out and begged him to talk to Augustine. But he refused. He said he could tell that Augustine was full of pride and that he loved arguments, and so he was not ready for an honest discussion.

He gave Monica an important insight about her son's character. Some people won't be convinced by an argument. They need to feel that they're figuring things out on their own. They may change their minds eventually, but only after they can chalk it up to their own thinking.

Monica didn't like this answer. She wanted to see Augustine change, and she wanted it now. Seeing her son put in his place would probably also have brought her a measure of satisfaction. Monica pleaded with the bishop, and would not let him go, until he, too, was at his wit's end. Losing patience, he assured her that it would not be possible for "the son of these tears" to be lost (*Confessions* 3.12.21).

That was enough. Monica took those words to be a prophecy, and she went on her way.

When seeking outside help, we should imitate Monica in her prudence. She recognized her limitations. She didn't know enough about Manichaeism to argue with her son, so she found someone who could. A little later, when she and Augustine arrived in Milan, she found a bishop who was her son's intellectual equal, St. Ambrose, who could flatter Augustine's intelligence even as he flattened his objections.

Monica had to do her homework. She probably had to ask around to find the right person to talk to, and then she had to be both daring and humble to ask advice and help from these people. Sometimes they rebuffed her.

In looking for outside help, she also had to give up some control. The first bishop (whose name we never find out) did not do what Monica asked. In fact, he taught Monica — and all of us — an important lesson: people have different learning styles. Some will respond to a private correction, but some will recoil and take it as an attack. It doesn't hurt to reflect on the ways that we ourselves have been corrected. Maybe we've responded best to a sharp rebuke from a grandfather. Maybe we learned best from a book — a book recommended to us by someone we love and trust.

Meditation

From St. Augustine

She believed in Christ, that before she departed this life, she would see me a Catholic believer.... Meanwhile You [O Lord] granted her another answer ... from a certain bishop. He had been reared in Your Church and was well versed in your books. This woman pleaded that he should agree to talk with me, refute my errors, unteach the evil things I had learned, and teach me good; for this he was in the habit of doing when he found people ready to receive it.

But he refused, very prudently, as I afterwards came to see. For he answered that I was still unteachable — that I was inflated with the novelty of the heresy, and that I had already confused various inexperienced persons with difficult questions, as she herself had informed him.

"But leave him alone for a time," he said. "Just pray to God for him; he will of himself, by reading, discover what that error is, and how great its impiety."

He disclosed to her that when he was very small his own mother, misguided, had given him over to Manicheans. He had not only read, but even copied out almost all of their books! He came to see — without argument or proof from anyone — how much that sect was to be shunned, and so he shunned it.

Still, she would not be satisfied, but repeated more earnestly her pleas, shedding abundant tears, that he would see and converse with me.

Vexed at her persistence, he exclaimed, "Go your way, and God bless you, for it is not possible that the son of these tears would be lost."

She often mentioned that answer in her conversations with me. She accepted it as though it were a voice from heaven.

— Confessions 3.12.21

Resolution

I will not rely on my own strength alone. I will seek help from others when I need it.

Prayer

O generous St. Monica, there is no sacrifice that your maternal heart would not make in order to satisfy divine justice. You waited patiently, day and night, for God's good time to come. The delay only made your prayer most earnest. Intercede for us, too, that we, too, may know the graces you knew: that we may love justice, pray earnestly, and live in joyful, confident hope. Amen.

Chapter 11

A Servant Spirit

On her birthday, one year when Nan was in her nineties, her children took her out to dinner at her favorite seafood restaurant. While she was enjoying her lobster tail, a gentleman approached from a table nearby. "You probably don't remember me," he began.

He had lived down the street from our family, a half-century before in the 1950s. His mother, a single parent, tried to cobble together a living for herself and her son. Some nights, he said, it looked like they would have no dinner. Then suddenly Nan would show up at the door with freshly baked bread and a couple portions of whatever was on her own table. He concluded by thanking her. He had led a good life because she had given him hope.

In the 1950s, Nan didn't have much, as Pop's wages reflected an unsteady local economy. (Mining had gone into steep decline after the war.) Yet she always had enough to give some away.

Monica is known, according to an old tradition, by the title "Mother of the Poor." She constantly gave of herself. She was a peacemaker among her friends and neighbors. As she crossed the sea, she gave comfort to the distraught passengers — and even the panicked sailors — as their boat seemed about to sink. She

87

was a tireless parishioner. Once, St. Ambrose and his congregation peacefully occupied a basilica in Milan to prevent its seizure by the military; Monica played her part by caring for all the frightened and beleaguered protesters; meanwhile, she herself subsisted (Augustine later recalled) on prayer. When living with Augustine and his friends in Cassiciacum, she made sure they didn't skip meals.

"She was well known for good works," was her son's understated way of summing up.

Surely it was therapeutic, and surely it's worthy of our imitation. When we find ourselves preoccupied by our own hurts and by the injustices visited upon us, it probably means we're not thinking enough about others. When we give ourselves over to service, and throw ourselves into the care of others, we forget ourselves for a time. If we do it long enough, we grow selfless — and happier, even if things don't always go our way.

Charity is the presence of God in the world. Augustine once wrote: "If you have seen charity, you have seen the Trinity." For the Trinity consists of three divine Persons, each giving himself entirely in love, holding nothing back.

That's the kind of love Monica showed her neighbors, even amidst her trials. That's the kind of love that will strengthen us as we grieve over our wayward children and pray for their return to the faith.

Meditation

From St. Augustine

She was also the servant of Your servants. Whoever knew her would praise, honor, and love You in her. Through the testimony of the fruits of holy conversation, they saw You were present in her heart. For she had been the wife of one man, had repaid her parents, and had guided her house devoutly. She was well known for good works. She had brought up children, and she labored to give birth to them (Galatians 4:19) whenever she saw them swerving from You. To all of us, O Lord ... she devoted care as if she had been mother of all; she served us as if she had been daughter of all.

— *Confessions* 9.9.22

Resolution

I will find opportunities to serve others and forget myself.

Prayer

A Litany of St. Monica

St. Monica, devout mother of St. Augustine, pray for us.

St. Monica, whose prayers won Augustine from sin, pray for us.

St. Monica, whose prayers gave Augustine to God, pray for us.

St. Monica, pattern for wives, pray for us.

St. Monica, model of mothers, and mother of saints, pray for us.

St. Monica, exemplar of widows, pray for us.

St. Monica, devoted to prayer, pray for us.

St. Monica, so patient in trials, pray for us.

St. Monica, so resigned in sorrow, pray for us.

St. Monica, so happy in death, pray for us.

St. Monica, devoted child of Mary, Mother of
Consolation, pray for us.

~~⌒~~

Chapter 12

Their Sufferings, Their Choices

Nan lived to be ninety-four. A life so long will see its share of sorrow, but nothing affected her so strongly as her children's suffering.

It is not easy for us to watch our children suffer, whether they are young children misunderstood by a teacher, teens outcast by a social group, young adults slogging through long days at a miserable job, or midlifers hitting a rough patch in marriage. Monica's heart surely ached for her idealistic son as he struggled to teach classrooms full of spoiled troublemakers. She suffered his disappointment, disillusion, and crisis of confidence.

He admits in the *Confessions* (5.8.14): "I didn't want to go to Rome because my friends, who talked me into it, promised me greater opportunities and honors there. I was *influenced* by these considerations, but my main and almost only motive was that I'd been told that young people studied more quietly there, and were kept under control with tougher discipline. So they didn't whimsically and arrogantly rush into the classroom of a teacher who was not their own — a place they were forbidden to enter without permission. At Carthage, on the contrary, the schoolboys had a shameful and intemperate freedom. They burst in rudely, with an almost furious manner. They interrupted the order that anyone may have established for the good of his pupils.... My mother grievously lamented my journey."

Monica objected. She ached for his sorrows. Yet she could not live his life for him. She could not make his choices for him. If she thought he was deciding badly, she let him know in no uncertain terms. She "grievously lamented" his journey. But she could not force his hand. She had to respect his freedom and trust that God would work even in less than optimal circumstances in her son's life.

When our children are very small, our parental authority is almost absolute. They need to be lifted or guided from one place to another. They cannot open the doors we close. We have the means to distract them from situations or friendships we don't approve of.

As they grow older, however, we find ourselves increasingly standing on the sidelines of their relationships. Though they may seek our advice or consolation, they don't want us to intervene in their social mix. In any event, direct parental intervention in social matters is often counterproductive. We can make things worse for our kids by trying too hard to make them better.

Monica knew that there was only so much she could do to direct the life of her son, now a young adult. Threats would be futile and alienating. She had to respect his freedom, even if she thought he was making a rash move. It's possible, too, that she recognized a selfish motive in her own heart. Perhaps she wanted him to forgo the new job because it could mean a permanent separation from her. She might never see him again. Such a prospect would certainly cloud a parent's judgment.

The words *sympathy* and *compassion* mean, at root, to share another's suffering. It's best for us to listen to our children's troubles, offer clear advice, pray for them, but still acknowledge our limitations. In the end, we must respect the freedom God gives them, even if we wish they would use it a different way.

Meditation

From St. Augustine

> The daughter of one of the caretakers of the Church's property had been drawn away by the other [Donatist] party, against the will of her parents, and baptized by them. She was living as a nun when her father wished to compel her by severe treatment to return to the Catholic Church. But I was unwilling that this woman, though her mind was so perverted, should be received by us unless by her own will, and the free exercise of judgment, she chose what is better. When the countryman began to try to compel his daughter to submit to his authority, I immediately forbade his using any such means.

> — *Letter 35.4*

Resolution

I will try today to listen to my children more than I talk to them.

Prayer

O God, You do not permit to perish even that which is self-destructive. From nothing You have created the world, which every eye sees to be most beautiful. I entrust everything to You, O wisest and best of Fathers, and I shall pray for it as You shall in good time advise me. This I ask of Your extreme kindness: that you convert me entirely to You, and that You allow nothing to prevent me as I make my way to You. O Monica, pray for my children, that they might overcome all obstacles that keep them from trusting in their heavenly Father. Amen.

Chapter 13

The Loving Gaze

Some children are especially sensitive, and for them Mom or Dad's facial expression is never in neutral. One of us has such a daughter, now grown into a lovely young woman. When she was a tot, she could hardly stand for a parental face to be without a smile. She'd ask, "Why are you angry?" when no one in the house was the least bit angry. If her parents weren't beaming, that raised an alarm for her. Something wasn't right with the world. The absence of a smile was equal to a frown.

It was an intuition about the fallen world — the world this side of heaven — that perhaps she shared with the older Augustine. As bishop, he once defined heaven simply as "looking upon one who looks back in love."

That's what we all want: to look upon someone who returns our gaze lovingly. That's the definition of heaven, but it's also foreshadowed on earth. We don't feed, as animals do. We have family meals, where we talk with one another and gaze at one another. It's not primarily about the food.

God created human nature with a bundle of instincts and biological drives, all calibrated to direct us toward the loving gaze. The so-called sex drive isn't satisfied by sex. It's satisfied when we look upon one who looks back in love. It's satisfied, down to our chemical components, when we gaze into the eyes of a spouse — and then satisfied still more deeply when we look upon the baby our love has conceived. Scientists note that newborns can see only the distance from the mother's breast to her eyes. They are built to look upon one who looks back in love.

Our faces should communicate that love. Small children, no matter their age, are especially sensitive to changes in the parental demeanor. They look into our eyes as they look into a mirror. In our expressions, they find their own self-worth. They know nothing about how the boss treated us for the last nine hours. They know only that they have succeeded in making you smile — or they've failed to make you smile. A daughter who reminds us to smile is a prophet sent by God.

Blessed Mother Teresa of Calcutta made this her constant refrain: "A smile is the beginning of love.... Peace begins with a smile. Smile five times a day at someone you don't really want to smile at at all. Do it for peace.... We can never know how much good a simple smile can do."

When we smile at family members, we are providing a foretaste of heaven.

On the other hand, our blank faces may seem to say, "You bore me," even though that's not our intention.

Smiles beget smiles. They're infectious. Smiles — even when they're mustered with much effort and interior struggle — are self-fulfilling prophecies. Our smiles make others smile, and then their smiles have a positive effect on us.

If we get in the habit of smiling, we'll find more reasons to smile as time goes on.

Here's the tough part. To do this right, we need to smile, as Mother Teresa said — and as Monica knew — at people who really don't make us feel like smiling.

We need to look with love upon those who have hurt us — and haven't apologized for it.

Upon those who have defamed us; those who have ignored us; our own children, perhaps, who haven't always treated us with due respect.

We need to look with love upon those whom we have resented — and those who have resented us; upon those whom we have failed to forgive; upon those whom we have envied; upon those whom we have despised, or who have despised us.

It's not optional. And it's not about justice. It's about looking upon another with the kind of mercy we want one day to know for ourselves and know without ceasing.

Meditation

From St. Augustine

What is the top in the design of that building we're constructing? How high will the highest point of this building reach? I say without hesitation: even to the vision of God. You see how high, how great a thing it is to see God. Whoever longs for it understands both what I say and what he hears. The vision of God is promised to us — of the true God, the supreme God. For this is the good, to see him who sees.

For those who worship false gods, see them easily; but they see those "who have eyes but ... see not" (Psalm 135:16). But to us is promised the vision of the living and the seeing God, that we may desire eagerly to see that God of whom Scripture says, "He who planted the ear, does he not hear? He who formed the eye, does he not see?" (Psalm 94:9). Does he then not hear, who has made for you the organ of your hearing, and does not he see, who has created the organ of your sight? ... Doesn't he fix his eye upon you, who made your eye? Out of nothing he created you and gave you being; and doesn't he care for you now that you are? ... He sees you, and there is no place where you can hide yourself from his eyes.

— *Sermon 19.3*

Resolution

I will make an effort to smile at others, especially those I find difficult.

Prayer

O Lord Jesus ... Look upon me that I may love You. Call me that I may see You and forever possess You. Monica, pray for me that my face, my hands, and the warmth of my voice might express to my children, always, the love within me for them. Amen.

Chapter 14

Guardian Angels

Through his years as a priest and bishop, Augustine spoke often of a devotion that he surely had learned from his mother: his devotion to the holy angels. It is a healthy devotion. It is a useful devotion for parents.

For every child has a guardian angel, present from conception onward. The angel is a "spiritual, non-corporeal" being (CCC 328) created by God for the purpose of getting *that particular child* to heaven. Angels are far more intelligent and powerful than we are. Their influence is subtle, but effective — though both we and our children still possess free will to resist even the greatest goods.

Augustine often describes our relationship with angels as "friendship" and "fellowship." Angels, unlike earthly friends, Augustine noted, will never let us down (see *City of God* 19.9).

That calls for prayerful devotion on our part. In another place Augustine wrote: "The truth counsels human beings to seek the fellowship of the holy angels" (*Letter* 102.19).

We should get to know not only our own guardian angels, but also those of our children. Angels are *messengers*. That's the literal meaning of the Greek word *angelos* — "messenger." Each angel was created by God for the purpose of communication. They have powers of persuasion that we lack. They can break through where we repeatedly fail. Moreover, they want the same things we want. They want the best for us and for our children.

The Church's tradition teaches us simple prayers to establish such friendship. Nan was passionately devoted to the guardian angels, and she passed that love along to her children as she taught them the simple rhyming prayer:

> *Angel of God, my guardian dear,*
> *To whom God's love entrusts me here:*
> *Ever this day be at my side*
> *To light and guard, to rule and guide. Amen.*

It's good for us to pray this prayer in the morning as we prepare for our day. But it's good also to go back to the guardian angels, our own and those of our children, often during the day. We should ask them to help especially when we need to say something that's difficult to put into words, something that could be taken the wrong way, something that might sting a little. The angels can help us find the right words, form the right facial expressions, and deliver the message in the best way possible. But they can also influence our children to receive the message in the best way possible. Listening is half the task of communication, and sometimes the more demanding half.

Devotion to the angels is a great secret we can learn from the Christians of Augustine's time. It is too much neglected today, when communications so often are broken down.

Meditation

From St. Augustine

> It was not for the angels that Christ died. Yet the re-
> demption of man through his death was in a sense
> accomplished for the angels. The enmity which sin
> had put between men and the holy angels is re-
> moved, and friendship is restored between them;
> and by the redemption of man the gaps which the
> great apostasy left in the angelic host are filled up.
>
> — *Handbook on Faith, Hope, and Love*, 61–62

Resolution

I will "visit," at least once a day, with the guardian angel
of one of my children.

Prayer

Watch, O Lord, with those who wake, or watch, or weep
tonight, and give Your angels charge over those who
sleep. Tend your sick ones, O Lord Christ. Rest Your
weary ones. Bless Your dying ones. Soothe Your suffering ones. Pity Your afflicted ones. Shield Your joyous
ones. And all for Your love's sake. Amen.

Chapter 15

Be Appreciative

Monica's husband Patricius was hardly the model spouse. He had some glaring faults. Augustine mentions his raging temper and his philandering.

Yet Monica managed to avoid bitterness, and she even raised her son to think kindly of his father and to appreciate the good things he did for the family. Augustine acknowledges his father's sins, but more often he mentions the sacrifices Patricius made so that his son could get the finest education.

We don't know where Augustine came by this habit of appreciating others, but we can bet he often heard it from his mother. We can bet that Monica often expressed gratitude and often said thank you — not only to God, but also to her beloved family. Augustine himself said: "When good things fall to our lot, we should not only congratulate ourselves, but show our gratitude to those to whom we owe them" (*Letter 15*).

One of the great obstacles to family communication is a shortage of gratitude. We live in the midst of a million blessings, and yet all we tend to think about it the one irritant *du jour*. We're like the professor in Nathaniel Hawthorne's story whose wife is perfect, he believes, except for one solitary blemish. He becomes obsessed with the blemish, and concocts a potion that removes it, with the unfortunate side-effect of killing his wife.

Let's not focus on the negatives in our relationships, but be grateful for the positives. Psychologists at the University of California have been conducting a long-term research project on gratitude. They concluded recently that gratitude is an "integral component of health, wholeness, and well-being."

Thankful people are happier people. And they make their homes happier and more communicative. Why? Because people who receive thanks feel appreciated and feel loved.

It can be helpful now and then to take a few minutes alone and do a "gratitude inventory" — make a list of the great qualities of each family member. We can keep that list in a wallet or purse and use it to offer a prayer of thanksgiving every day.

Gratitude is the necessary precondition of communication and communion. Did you know that the Greek root of the word Eucharist, *Eucharistia*, means "thanksgiving"? God doesn't need our gratitude, but he knows that we need to be grateful, so he made our greatest earthly fulfillment to be a great act of thanksgiving.

The lesson for our homes should be clear. If we say thank you often, we'll make life a lot more heavenly.

Meditation

From St. Augustine

I give thanks to our God and Lord, because of the hope and faith and love which are in You; and I thank You, in Him, for thinking so well of me as to believe me to be a faithful servant of God, and for the love which with guileless heart You cherish towards all that You commend in me…. To You I also render many thanks for this, that You encourage me wonderfully to aspire after such excellence, by Your praising me as if I had already attained it. Many more thanks still shall be Yours, if you not only claim an interest in my prayers, but also cease not to pray for me. For intercession on behalf of a brother is more acceptable to God when it is offered as a sacrifice of love.

— *Letter 20, to Antoninus*

Resolution

I will say thank you more often, to God and to others.

Prayer

We glorify You, O Lord, we praise You, we give You thanks; for by Your Spirit we are led to do such things that show us to be the children of God. "For all who are led by the Spirit of God are [children] of God" (Romans 8:14). Monica, pray for me that I approach my children in a spirit of gratitude, thanking God for the gift they are to me.

Chapter 16

Salvation and Ecstasy

As Augustine dawdled on his way to the Church, his last stop was among the philosophical school of Platonists in Milan. Some of its members were Christian, and others were not. Today we refer to the fourth-century movement as "Neo-Platonism." It was based on the ideas of Plato, who had lived in the fourth century before Christ, but the new school had accumulated many religious ideas and esoteric practices. Its goal was union with "the one," a vague and somewhat impersonal conception of God.

Some of the leading lights of Neo-Platonism had lived a century before. The big names were Plotinus and his student Porphyry. Both men had probably received some Christian instruction, but veered away from Christ before they could be baptized.

Through disciplined meditation and study, they sought union with the divine. They worked at it. Yet the great master, Plotinus, had reached this goal just a few times in the course of his life, and only after a great effort, and only for fleeting moments. And then it was gone. Porphyry only got there once.

This did not hold out much hope for other Neo-Platonists — never mind the great masses of humanity, many of whom could not read and did not have the leisure for meditation and study.

It seemed a small sort of salvation: a few people might — just might — unite themselves, for a negligible amount of time, to a deity who couldn't care less about them.

Augustine came to see his mother in stark contrast to these philosophers. Indeed he came to revere her, he said, as a master of philosophy, and he pledged himself as her student.

She could not read Plotinus or Porphyry. She probably couldn't read much more than the signs put out by the grocer. She did not practice strange meditation techniques. She went to Mass. She listened to the Gospels that were read in church. She sang hymns and psalms. And she wept to God as she prayed.

Yet Monica accomplished what the great masters could not. She arrived at a deep communion with the One. It was lasting, not fleeting. And it wasn't something she achieved by way of effort, but rather something she received as a grace.

We, too, will accomplish more if we give first priority to our own relationship with God. We cannot give away what we don't first possess. Jesus himself said it well: What good is it if we gain the whole world, yet forfeit our soul (see Mark 8:36)? We need to grow in the life of prayer, and then model a life of prayer that's attractive to others. If our children see joy, they'll want what we have. If they see misery, they won't. Misery may love company, but it also repels the company it craves.

What attracted Augustine about his mother's way of salvation — Jesus' way of salvation — was that it brought lasting serenity here on earth, even in the midst of great trials. That's what he wanted. It's what everybody wants.

Scholars say that Augustine wanted to communicate this message to the world, and that his telling of the "ecstasy at Ostia" — when he and Monica felt, as they discussed heaven, that they were swept momentarily out of themselves — is modeled after Neo-Platonist accounts of the ascent of the soul. It is credible and persuasive. This side of heaven, we'll never know how many readers have read that account and found there what they had long sought in dead-end places. Such ecstasy simply cannot be found in strange occult practices and obscure academic philosophy.

Meditation

From St. Augustine

The day was coming when she would leave this life. (You knew that day; we did not.) It happened — and I believe You arranged it by Your secret ways — that she and I were standing alone, leaning in the window. We could see the garden of the house in Ostia where we were staying, resting for the trip away from the crowd after the fatigue of a long journey. We were talking very pleasantly alone, "forgetting what lies behind and straining forward to what lies ahead" (Philippians 3:13); we were trying to figure out together — in the presence of the Truth, which you are — what kind of life the eternal life of the saints would be, which "no eye has seen, nor ear heard, nor the heart of man conceived" (1 Corinthians 2:9). We opened wide the mouth of our heart to the celestial streams of your fountain, the fountain of life — which is with you — so that, sprinkled with it according to our capacity, we might somehow consider such a deep mystery.

Our conversation reached the point where the very highest pleasure of the bodily senses, even in the very brightest material light, seemed not only unworthy of comparison, but unworthy even of mentioning, because of the sweetness of that life of the saints. Lifting ourselves up with a more burning affection towards that life, we gradually passed through all bodily things, and even the heaven itself from which the sun, moon, and stars shine down on earth.

We soared even higher by our inner meditation and talking and admiring your works. We came to our own minds and went beyond them. We rose up as high as that region of unfailing plenty where you feed Israel forever with the food of truth, and where life is that Wisdom by whom all these things are made — the things that have been, and the things that are to come. And that Wisdom is not made, but she is as she has been and will always be....

While we were talking that way, and straining after her, we slightly touched her with the whole effort of our heart. We sighed, and left the first-fruits of the spirit bound there.

— *Confessions* 9.10.23–24

Resolution

I will tend to my own spiritual life in the first place, gaining more for myself of what I hope to share with my children.

Prayer

O God, framer of the universe, grant me first rightly to invoke You; then to show myself worthy to be heard by You; and lastly set me free. O Monica, pray that I keep heaven in mind as I pray for my children, especially those who have strayed from the truth. Amen.

Chapter 17

Nothing Is Far from God

As Monica lay dying in Ostia, her sons expressed anxiety that they would not be able to return her body to be buried in Africa. In their culture it was considered a terrible misfortune to die in a place where no family could visit your grave. Monica laughed away their fears. "Nothing," she said, "is far from God."

Through the ordeal of her son's adulthood, she had learned to trust God. Yes, she had done heroic and extraordinary things, traveled far to be near her son. But she came to know that even when Augustine was far from God, God was not far from Augustine.

There comes a time when children range far from their parents, but they are never far from their Father God, and he has a plan for them. Certainly their parents are part of that plan. Parents will continue to love their children, counsel them, console them, and cook for them, whenever these things are possible. But when they're not possible, God is still there, even in the most remote places. If our children fly to the heavens, go underground, or fly to the uttermost parts of the sea, they are never far from God (see Psalm 139). "No place is far from God."

Even the darkness of the darkest lives is light to almighty God. Long after the life of St. Monica, another saint, St. John Vianney (1786–1859), consoled a widow whose husband had committed suicide, saying: "Between the bridge and the water, there was God."

God does not abandon his children. He does not abandon *our* children. We may not know the satisfaction, in this life, of seeing our children secure in a good place. But we can learn to trust, as Monica learned, and so we must. We can learn to hope, as Monica did, and so we must.

Meditation

From St. Augustine

She was laid low by a fever; and one day while she was sick, she fainted and fell briefly unconscious. We rushed over to her; but she soon regained her senses, and gazing on me and my brother as we stood by her, she said to us, "Where was I?" Then looking intently at us speechless with grief, she said, "You shall bury your mother here." I was silent, and held back from weeping; but my brother said something to the effect that he wished, for her sake, that she could die in her native land and not abroad.

When she heard this, she looked at him with an anxious expression, and then gazing at me she said, "See how he speaks!" Then to both of us she said, "Lay this body anywhere. Don't trouble yourself at all with its care. This only I ask, that you will remember me at the Lord's altar, wherever you may be." And when she had said this as best she could, she fell silent, in pain with her increasing sickness....

I recalled how she had ever burned with anxiety about her burial place, which she had provided and prepared for herself by the body of her husband. For they had lived very peacefully together. And so little is the human mind capable of grasping things divine that she wished also for this to be added to their happiness. She wanted people to say that, after her wandering beyond the sea, it had been granted her that two who were so united on earth should rest together in the same grave....

But this uselessness had, through the bounty of [God's] goodness, left her heart, and I was full of joy admiring what she had thus disclosed to me.... I heard afterwards, too, that while we were at Ostia, with a maternal confidence she one day, when I was absent, was speaking with my friends on the contempt of this life and the blessing of death. They were amazed at the courage [God] had given to a woman, and asked her whether she did not dread leaving her body so far away from her own city. She replied, "Nothing is far from God. I have no fear that he won't know where to find me when he comes to raise me at the end of the world."

— *Confessions* 9.11.27–28

Resolution

I will strive to praise God and hope in him serenely, even if I do not see earthly fulfillment of my prayers.

Prayer

Hear me, graciously hear me, my God, my Lord, my King, my Father, my Cause, my Hope, my Wealth, my Honor, my House, my Country, my Health, my Light, my Life. From now on, I love You alone. You alone I seek. You alone am I prepared to serve, for You alone are Lord who is worthy of the title. I want to be in Your dominion. Direct, I pray, and command whatever You will, but heal and open my ears, that I may hear Your words. Heal and open my eyes, that I may behold the signs of Your command. Drive all illusions from me, that I may recognize You. O Monica, pray with me that God will heal and open the ears and eyes of my children to the love of God, beyond all measure. Amen.

Chapter 18

Our Intercessor

Particular devotions usually arise within the Church from the experience of common people. No one knows the author of the *Memorare* prayer. It appeared rather suddenly and spread like wildfire among the faithful. No one knows why devotion to St. Jude, as the patron of "lost causes," became a devotional fixture some nineteen centuries or so after the death of the Apostle.

The Holy Spirit draws God's faithful people together. The Holy Spirit is the bond of unity in the Church. But the Spirit is also the bond of unity in Christian friendships. It is God Himself who draws the hearts of Christians in devotion to particular saints. It is God Himself who has drawn many, many parents to look to St. Monica for help and intercession for the sake of their children.

Here as always, grace builds on nature. It's only natural that we should look to her. She has run the race of parenting. For her it was a hard race, but she has won, and she won by means of her prayer.

Consider her son's testimonials to his mother's intercessory power:

My rescue was granted because of the faithful and daily tears of my mother, that I should not perish. (*On the Predestination of the Saints*, 2:53)

To her merits I owe all that I am. (*Happy Life*, 1.6)

Your handmaid brought me forth in her flesh, so that I might be born to this temporal light, and in her heart, so that I might be born to life eternal. (*Confessions*, 9.8.17)

Your faithful one, my mother, wept to you on my behalf more than mothers weep over the bodily death of their children. For she saw that I was dead to that faith and spirit which she had from You. And You heard her, O Lord. You heard her, and despised not her tears when, pouring down, they watered the earth under *her eyes in every place where she prayed. Yes, You heard her.* (*Confessions*, 3.11.19)

Monica had to wait and pray for many years. It's not that God wasn't listening. It's not that God didn't love her enough. In the course of his *Confessions*, Augustine emphasizes that God delayed the answer for Monica's own good. By waiting she learned to trust God. She learned to be detached from earthly results, but hopeful for heavenly ends. The long wait purified Monica of all the earthbound reasons for raising such a prayer: shame over her son's public sins ... the desire for human esteem and admiration ... the hankering to have a child she could brag about.

Through seventeen years of prayer and suffering, Monica allowed God to smooth out the rough spots in her character and prepare her for life with him in heaven. By grace, she spent her years on earth improving her skills at intercession, and it purified her. It was a purgatory for her, burning away her pride and anger, and anything that might keep her from God.

It is no wonder she gained the reputation for patronage of parents, especially those whose children have strayed.

In the Middle Ages, as the Augustinian monks conveyed her body to its new home in Rome, people in the streets shouted, "It's Augustine's mother! It's Augustine's mother!" The chronicles record that many people were moved to invoke her intercession as she passed by. Two miracles were recorded, and both were healings begged by mothers on behalf of their children. ·

In modern times the devotion to St. Monica has been promoted by popes and bishops, but its true energy comes from parents, especially mothers.

Meditation

From St. Augustine

I received the scourge of bodily sickness, and I was descending into hell burdened with all the sins that I had committed against You, myself, and others.... The fever increasing, I was now passing away and perishing.... She was ignorant of this, yet, while absent, prayed for me. You, who are present everywhere, listened to her where she was, and had pity upon me where I was, that I should regain my bodily health, although still frenzied in my sacrilegious heart....

I cannot sufficiently express the love she had for me, nor how she now labored for me in the spirit with a far keener anguish than when she bore me in the flesh.

— *Confessions* 5.9.16

Resolution

I will trust God if he makes me wait for what I want. He wants to make me a saint.

Prayer

May St. Augustine and his mother, St. Monica, accompany us with their prayers and draw us ever closer to the Lord.

— Pope Benedict XVI, General Audience,
August 25, 2010

Conclusion

The Hope of Ostia

Ostia Antica is just a short bus ride from Rome, if you travel on a weekend or holiday. There you are free to walk the very streets that Augustine and his mother walked during the last weeks of Monica's life. The paving stones are still the same. The baths Augustine visited on the day of his mother's funeral are in pretty good shape, for their age. Some of the walls of the basilica — where Monica's body was probably laid out — are still intact.

What was once the bustling port of the capital of the world is now a vast archeological site. Shortly after Monica died and Augustine sailed back to Africa, the barbarians took Italy, and Ostia fell under a spell, like a kingdom in the fairy tale. Only in the last few years has it been excavated, drawn out of more than a millennium of silt and sand. Today, Ostia Antica is a state-run park, owned and operated by the Italian government.

Yet for those who know the story, it is holy ground. For those who have suffered with their children — and suffered because of their children and suffered for their children — it is a pilgrimage destination. They walk the empty streets, overgrown with weeds, and wonder: "Could this have been the house?" And they look into the windows for answers, for direction, and for hope.

The story of Monica and her son Augustine is a story of hope. She was an extraordinary woman, but she experienced the graces God offers to everyone.

John Paul I was pope for the briefest moment, for a month in 1978, and he had time to meet with pilgrims in only four general audiences. On one of those Wednesdays the smiling pope told the story of the last days of Monica and Augustine.

> On the seashore at Ostia, in a famous conversation, Augustine and Monica, "forgetting the past and turning to the future, asked themselves what eternal life would be." This is Christian hope ... and what we intend when we pray, with the catechism: *My God, I hope from your goodness ... eternal life and the necessary graces to deserve it with good works, which I must do and want to do. My God, let me not remain confounded for ever.* (Pope John Paul I, General Audience, September 20, 1978)

It is a most beautiful scene, and Pope Benedict XVI echoed the teaching of his predecessor.

> By then St. Monica had become for this son of hers, "more than a mother, the source of his Christianity." For years her one desire had been the conversion of Augustine, whom she then saw actually turning to a life of consecration at the service of God. She could therefore die happy, and in fact she passed away on 27 August 387, at the age of

56, after asking her son not to trouble about her burial but to remember her, wherever he was, at the Lord's altar. St. Augustine used to say that his mother had "conceived him twice." (Pope Benedict XVI, Sunday Angelus Address, August 30, 2009)

We, too, hope that we have conceived our children "twice," once by means of ordinary human love and yet again as we carried or led them to the baptismal font. Perhaps we are still leading, or still carrying, though it sometimes seems we are stumbling in the dark. We must go forward in prayer, as Monica did, that the children of our tears may not perish, and trust that for almighty God even the darkness is light.

Pope Benedict is a devoted scholar of St. Augustine, and so he returns to the story of St. Monica again and again:

May St. Augustine obtain the gift of a sincere and profound encounter with Christ for all those young people who, thirsting for happiness, are seeking it on the wrong paths and getting lost in blind alleys.

St. Monica and St. Augustine invite us to turn confidently to Mary, Seat of Wisdom. Let us entrust Christian parents to her so that, like Monica, they may accompany their children's progress with their own example and prayers. Let us commend youth to the Virgin Mother of God so that, like Augustine, they may always strive for the fullness of Truth and Love which is Christ: he alone can satisfy the deepest desires of the human heart. (Pope Benedict XVI, Sunday Angelus Address, August 27, 2006)

Recommended Reading

Aquilina, Mike, and Christopher Bailey, *Mothers of the Church: The Witness of Early Christian Women* (Huntington, IN: Our Sunday Visitor, 2012).

St. Augustine, *Confessions*, translated by R.S. Pine-Coffin (New York: Penguin, 1961).

St. Augustine, *My Mother*, edited John E. Rotelle, O.S.A. (Villanova, PA: Augustinian Press, 1987).

Falbo, Giovanni, *St. Monica: The Power of a Mother's Love* (Boston: Pauline, 2007).

Fitzgerald, Allan D., editor, *Augustine through the Ages: An Encyclopedia* (Grand Rapids, MI: 1999).

O'Meara, John J., *The Young Augustine: The Growth of Augustine's Mind up to His Conversion* (London: Longmans, 1954).